For Trees So Tall

Praise For "For Trees So Tall"

"Exquisitely written, incredibly compelling, I could not put it down!"

Erika Christopher, Literary Consultant

"I laugh, I cry...I hold her in Spirit for having gigantic balls, bigger than mine! It's beautiful."

Tim Brogdan, Musician

"For Trees So Tall reminded me of what it feels like to have true connection in our spirit—to nature, each other, and God. If anyone is in search of more enlightenment through struggle, peace in an over-stimulated world, and hope in overcoming, this book is a must read. Beautifully written, thought provoking, and so looking forward to book #2!!"

Jennifer Cleary, Entrepreneur & Owner of The Wandering

You are about to read the life story of my friend Jess.

Because of her moment-to-moment acceptance of her life's story as she has experienced it and because of her intentional volition to purposefully alchemize her experience into power and resource, purpose and hope…. one can only conclude that the rest of us…the rest of us blessed to be alive human beings…can hope to open our eyes and be awake and aware.

You might expect a punchline. You might expect a poetic resolution at the termination and conclusion of her words. You might expect a ribbon-wrapped message of equative "how-to."

….and you will have missed the point of my friend's grace and courage. I beg you to be brave and open. My friend Jess's words are …uninhibitedly …. in grace.

It isn't always pretty and it isn't always perfect…in fact rarely so. If anything, love is most perfect when held within the misunderstood pathos of imperfection.

…Jess…I am so blessed, as we all are, for your naked courage as I still know that in a million years you would never even be tempted to define it as such…..have patience and compassion for the rest of us.

Much Love,
Tim Brogdon
Pittsburgh, 2021

Gratitude

I could not have written this book without the loving support of my family, most of all, my husband Doug. He stepped up in countless ways to ensure I had the space to write and took on the all-important job of editor, sharing tears and triumphs in the process.

I am grateful to my mess of a maternal family who brought me strife but also tremendous gifts. Hillis may have chosen the mountains to make money, but in doing so he gave me the opportunity to grow up in one of the most beautiful places on earth.

Speaking of the earth, this book is essentially for her, for all of us and our connection with her and the Spirit that connects us all. Tremendous gratitude for the trees, streams, mountains, and dirt that feed my soul every day, may this book remind others of your invaluable gifts and invite them to be curious about you. Only when we remember our connection to you and the wonder that you are will, we choose to live our lives in greater balance.

Equally deserved gratitude to: Stephanie Pierucci, the firecracker and facilitator, Kathy Denson, who despite herself, never stopped believing in me and Faren Wilbur who saw my vision and brought it to fruition for the book cover, you are a beautiful and talented soul! To Erin Rigney, Sarah Uhl, Jen Cleary, Lindsay Gurley, Eden Marsh and all the women artists and creatives who create something out of nothing... you inspire me every day, thank you. Thank you to Jules, Pixie and Dez for listening to me talk about this process for so long! And tremendous gratitude to Julie Wagner...for being my biggest fan, your belief in me is humbling.

To my children, who give me humor, grace, wisdom, and clumsiness all in the same breath. I would be lost without you, thank you for choosing to walk this life with me.

Gratitude and giggles to Paul's Boxers (and Paul), you know who you are, your love and encouragement helped me believe in myself and kept me going on hard days. As always, I am finishing strong!

And gratitude to the process of writing itself, it brought forth tremendous healing.

Finally, immense gratitude to Spirit, this book would not have been written without the guidance of Spirit and my spirit guides for whom I am grateful for everyday that I can feel and hear them as they move with me through life...

With love and light,
Jess

Cataloguing in publication information is
Available from Library and Archives U.S.
ISBN 978-1-956257-11-3
Pierucci Publishing
www.Pieruccipublishing.com

Edited by Doug Jacobson
Printed and Bound by Amazon.com

JessJacobson

#motherearth
#earthhealing

PIERUCCI PUBLISHING

We're Publishing!

Are you a writer, visionary, activist, business owner, healer, or thought leader who is eager to step up as a leader in today's great awakening?

Pierucci Publishing is now accepting applications for new authors.

If you feel inspired to write, publish, or market a bestselling book, please visit us at www.PierucciPublishing.com. You may also call or text us at 855-720-1111, or email us at Support@PierucciPublishing.com.

"When you go out into the woods, and you look at trees, you see all these different trees. And some of them are bent, and some of them are straight, and some of them are evergreens, and some of them are whatever. And you look at the tree and you allow it. You see why it is the way it is. You sort of understand that it didn't get enough light, and so it turned out that way. And you don't get all emotional about it. You just allow it. You appreciate the tree. The minute you get near humans, you lose all that. And you are constantly saying "you are too this or I am to this." That judgment mind comes in. And so, I practice turning people into trees. Which means appreciating them just the way they are."

- Ram Dass

Table of Contents

Dear Reader,

FOR TREES SO TALL is a layered memoir of generational trauma and interconnected truths. Two distinct paths; one of suffering, the other of courage and light. Walk these paths with me and see your own dark and light. Like the trees of the forest; we bend, we twist, we grow, weathering the storms...always reaching for the light.

This book has been lovingly written to help you embrace the natural world around you for inspiration, enlightenment, and healing.

With this intention in mind, I have recorded a Yoga Nidra for you, The Medicine Tree. Lie back, close your eyes, relax your body, and allow my words to guide you in a healing meditation.

Please download our audio Yoga Nidra free at www.Fortreessotall.com or scan this code with your phone to be directed to the web page.

In love and light,

Jess Jacobson
Carbondale, Colorado
September 2021

Chapter One

The Nature of Connection

It was the summer of 1977, ankle deep in a Colorado mountain stream where my love of nature was born. I came to this place while taking refuge, I had visited this spot many times before, but never for this long. It was my safe place, where the trees kept me company, dancing in the wind, making music with their leaves and whispering the secrets of the ancients. I listened to their stories as I built fairy houses out of worn river rocks, small sticks, and wildflowers. This is the only place I wanted to be, I was part of something bigger than myself and I sank into the creek bed like it was my home, like I belonged, like I too was a tree.

How long have I been here? I wondered, I was getting hungry, the air was cooling off now and the light was giving way to shadow. My skin was pink from the hot sun; had it not been for the mud I plastered all over my body I would have looked more like a tomato than a peach. I loved the feel of the mud drying against my skin, pulling tight before it cracked and began to crumble away. I often helped it along by plunging my whole body into the creek, letting the current carry away my protective layer in a brown cloud all at once. I did this over and over again, never tiring of the ritual.

The water carried its own secrets, the story of creation and the connection of life. I understood the fluidity of its language, where it came from and where it was going. Perhaps not in my mind, but in my body and soul; a reflection of pure consciousness, completeness, and oneness.

The accessibility to the creek came as an unintended consequence of the confluence of man and nature. A new pedestrian bridge meant to connect our giant apartment complex to the bike path that led up to "the village" had recently been built. Great chunks of earth were gouged from the land to make way for the cement footings and steel beams that were to support the bridge. When the work was done, there still remained raw earth on either side allowing me to carve a trail down to the water.

Over time, the creek, conspiring with, or perhaps at the instance of the rhythms of nature, found the path of least resistance. Winding down the mountainside, feeding the land and its inhabitants before meeting its sister rivers and distant tributaries, eventually becoming one with the mighty Colorado River.

Hunger began to steal my attention away from my surroundings, so I decided it was time to head home. Climbing up out of the creek bed sometimes required I was on all fours, leaning into the hill, grabbing onto roots, and reaching for anything that might help me get over the lip. Once my head popped up above the wide expanse of grass that bordered the apartment complex serving as the transition from the man-made world to the natural one, I was home free.

Upon getting both feet on the grass I made an effort to brush off the dirt and mud that still remained on my body before returning home through the sliding glass door. As I got closer to our ground level apartment, I could hear the music blaring through the closed door. Despite it being a beautiful evening, the people gathered at our apartment remained inside.

I was nervous as I approached the door. *Did she remember to make me dinner?* I wondered.

I cracked open the door and slid through sideways, trying not to be noticed while scanning the room for my mom. She was easy to spot, the center of attention as always; this time she stood by the small round dining table in the corner with random people gathered around her. Sitting on the center of the table was a big pile of white powder. It reminded me of when my grandmother made homemade noodles and laid the flour out on the counter, waiting for the eggs. I knew better though, tonight there wasn't going to be a big warm plate of beef and noodles, tonight I was going to be lucky to eat at all.

Should I try to get her attention or just go straight for the refrigerator? I wondered. I went for the fridge, hoping there was something I could eat.

I found a packet of chipped beef left over from last night's dinner, "*Shit on a Shingle*" and a carton of milk with a few swigs left. It was better than nothing, so I sat on the floor against the kitchen wall next to the fridge, eating the meat right out of the blue and white packaging while drinking the rest of the milk straight from the carton. It didn't take long to finish, and I was still hungry when it was gone, but I knew tonight...*this was all there was going to be.*

I decided to go to my room in hopes of escaping the ever-present drone of Don Hennley and Glenn Frye, I swear *The*

Eagles and *Fleetwood Mac* were all they ever listened to.

A few people recognized me as I made my way through the crowd to my bedroom, "Hi Jessica!" came a far too enthusiastic greeting from Natalie, a woman my mom knew from town.

"Hi." I said back while staring at her wild eyes that seemed far too big for her face.

Upon entering my room, I find two people I don't think I know naked and rolling around together on my twin mattress that lay on the floor, they don't even notice me as I stand there wondering what to do next. I watch their bodies move for a moment before deciding to head back down to the water, but I will need a sweater, it's getting cold.

I am not quiet as I open my closet door to try and find something warm to wear. They stop and look at me for only a moment before laughing hysterically and deciding my presence makes no difference to them and continue their naked adventure. I grab what I need and get out of there.

I exhale as I close the sliding glass door behind me and walk out onto the grass under the night sky. *Thank God,* I think...*Now what?*

It was really getting dark now and I wasn't sure if I wanted to go down to the creek, but with nowhere else to go, it was my best option. Just as I reached the top of the trail, I heard my Uncle Alan call for me, "Jess.... Jessica! Are you out here? Time to come home honey."

Reluctantly, I turned around...*perhaps he will get me some more dinner,* I hoped.

The next day was no different than the one before, my mom would be asleep for hours to come, so I got dressed and ready to head down to the creek. Just as I was leaving, my Aunt Linda surprised me by bringing my two younger cousins over to play and make a big breakfast. She had a brown paper bag full of groceries and I wondered if my Uncle Alan had told her food was scarce around here.

"Jessica honey, why don't you take your cousins down to the creek with you while I make breakfast," my Aunt Linda suggested. "Here boys, just in case you find anything you want to keep." She handed them each an old jelly jar with a lid that had holes poked through it.

I loved my cousins, but I hated when they came to the creek with me. I liked to be still, careful, and watchful but they liked to be big, loud, and messy...they scared all my nature friends away.

When I was alone at the creek, I liked to disguise myself in mud and lay on the creek bed as still as possible and watch the frogs. Most amazing to me was their ability to be still and present while having total awareness of what was happening around them, giving them the ability to catch an insect in an unforeseen instant. This was an impossible task with my cousins around.

Instead, I shuddered as my cousins chased dragonflies, grasshoppers and crickets trying to catch them for their jar. Once they caught them, they were forgotten and left to die in the hot sun. *How careless,* I thought, *to sacrifice life for the temporary pleasure of dominance.*

This was to be expected, my cousins Jeremey four and Brad three were testing their boundaries and station in life. I was five now and had spent time with these creatures and knew them to be more than simply "at our disposal" and I said as much every time the boys captured something. I kept an eye on the jars and once we got them back to the apartment, I set the creatures free if I got a chance.

We returned from the water to the smell of bacon, I started salivating before I got in the door. It had been at least two days without a proper meal.

"Here you go honey," said my aunt as she handed me a plate of bacon and pancakes with sliced bananas.

"Thank you!" I said with big eyes as I went to sit on the floor in front of the sliding glass door.

We all sat together on the floor and ate our meal, my aunt visibly upset there were no chairs for the dining table. After breakfast my aunt took me into the kitchen to show me what she had brought over for me in the brown bag.

"Jessica, I put some food in this lower cupboard so you can reach it ok." There were a couple of cans of soup, macaroni and cheese, cereal, peanut butter, jelly, and bread.

"Do you know how to use a can opener? You will need it for the soup...Jesus Jessica, do you know if you have a can opener?" She was overwhelmed with what wasn't there.

"Yes, we have a can opener, it's in that drawer with the silverware." I say confidently to help her feel better.

"Ok honey, I also got you a gallon of milk, cheese, hotdogs and orange juice." She got down on her knees and took a hold of my shoulders, "Jessica, I know it's not a lot, but it should get you through a week or so. I am sorry I can't do more but I will come check on you in a few days ok...and you can always ask Uncle Alan for help too, ok."

"Ok." I felt like she thought things were worse than they were. I mean yes, I often didn't have enough food, but that is what I knew.

Snowmass Village is 9 miles outside of Aspen, tucked up into the mountains. The village or mall as it is sometimes called, is built on a steep mountainside that has been carved out like terraced rice fields to make way for parking, hotels, restaurants and bars, there is very little in the way of horizontal expanse.

Cocaine was a lifestyle for my mom, not a party drug, which meant it was best for me to be out of the way as often as possible. I didn't mind, I enjoyed the creek far more than our tiny apartment anyway. We had very little furniture and I certainly didn't have many toys or a TV to hold my attention.

The white lines that covered old album covers seemed to be the main focus of everyone who walked through the door. It was what I had to compete most with for attention; unfortunately, the white powder stole the show every time.

One day I asked, "Mom, what is all that white stuff?"

"It's my medicine sweetie, it's not for you ok, it's medicine. It could make you really sick."

"It doesn't seem like medicine." My brilliant five-year-old mind was calling her out.

"This is mommy's medicine Jessica, you stay clear, ok."

"Ok." I said, hanging my head, eyes to the floor.

One Good Leg

The cold clear water that I spent my days in was the result of melting snowpack from the iconic mountains that towered over us and drew thousands of people here every year to ski.

The town was aptly named Snowmass and like many before me, this is where I learned to ski.

At three years old, Snowmass was my introduction to the mountains and my doorway into the natural world. We had come from Des Moines by way of a brief stint in California.

The whole of my mom's family traveled to Colorado together in 1976 with the exception of her mother, Annette. My mom's dad, Hillis, led the excursion in an effort to get his new fur business off the ground.

He had enlisted his four kids to help him: crazy Uncle Harlan (Har), Uncle Alan (Stretch), Aunt Linda and my mom, Kathy. They were all young, still teenagers, some carrying the weight of children; each one eager to change their fortune and get out of Iowa.

Hillis's vision for a family run fur business came to fruition here, in the heart of Colorado, where the rich and famous came to play and spend their money.

I was four years old when my Uncle Alan or "Stretch" as he was affectionately called, took me to the mountain for the first time. He was the ultimate ski bum, working for the ski company running a snowcat at night so he could ski all day. He was the perfect teacher; his main goal was that I had a good time. Rather than consider my age a liability, he saw it as an opportunity to show me the kind of freedom he hadn't found until he was a teenager when he first found these mountains.

Once I understood the basics, mostly how to stop, Alan took me through every kind of terrain; steep, bumpy, powder, it didn't matter, we did it together. Perhaps it was because I was small and so close to the ground that I wasn't intimidated by the steepness or the bumps...or perhaps it was because he believed in me. It's hard to know if it was ignorance or intention, but he showed me freedom without fear, and I believed I was capable of skiing anything he was.

I got comfy on skis and with my surroundings by the time I was five and would often head out on my own. My mom's fur shop was positioned on the front end of the mall across from John Denver's iconic Tower Restaurant, not far from the ski hill. This made it easy for me to ski a couple runs without much adult supervision. I would ski lap after lap on The Big Burn and Fanny Hill before breaking for lunch at The Deli, where my dad, Dana worked as a line cook. My mom and dad were divorced but he followed us out to Colorado to stay close to me.

The Deli was right next to the mountain on the opposite end of the mall from my mom's shop. It was like my parents were the bookends of the mall, as long as I was somewhere within walking distance, I was good to cruise around on my own. It would have been an idyllic childhood had it not been for all the cocaine and the unintended consequences that it brought.

Sometimes my dad would come skiing with me, he only had one "good" leg after he lost his left leg just below the knee in a motorcycle accident when I was two, but that didn't stop him from skiing. There was a veterans office stationed in Snowmass Village and they were able to outfit him with skis on his poles giving him the necessary stability to ski on one leg. He looked like a human tripod flying down the hill in his denim jeans with one pant leg tied up around his stump, so it didn't drag in the snow.

My dad was a free man when he skied, I imagine it felt similar to riding his Harley; the wind in his long blond hair, a set of mirrored sunglasses and a shit eatin' grin on his face.

This was the best version of my dad and I loved being up on the mountain with him.

After one such ski day we headed back to The Deli where he worked, for some french fries. While we were eating, he said, "You want to see some people freak the fuck out?"

"I don't know." I answered a little nervously, afraid of what he might do.

He then proceeded to stick a ketchup packet under his pants and over his "fake leg." Without a second thought he pulled out his knife and stabbed himself, right into the ketchup and started screaming! Soon his scream turned to hysterical laughter, he thought he was the funniest guy around. I can't even remember what happened next, if anyone came rushing over or what, but even though I am laughing at his insanity now, I am sure at five years old it had to be a little traumatic, even if hilarious.

In The Beginning

My mother is the third of four children born in a small town in Iowa in 1957. She was born to a poor family that moved to the big city of Des Moines in search of prosperity. Soon though, her family splintered apart due to her father, Hillis' infidelity and further lack of discernment that eventually landed him in jail for mail fraud.

My mother, Kathleen, is most like her older brother, Harlan, both headstrong and willful but crazy in slightly different ways. Harlan was born with a birth defect that left him with severe joint pain and a strangely proportioned body with a small hunch in his back. Due to this as well as being the first born, he was always out to prove himself to the world and to his father. My mother was similar in that she also craved her father's approval and the two of them lived with an unspoken but understood rivalry for their father's affection.

Linda, the oldest girl, is the steadiest of the four kids, she is kind and motherly, intelligent but not a showoff. Last of all there was Alan, he is the youngest, tall, and skinny, taking after his dad, with a long face and piercing blue eyes. Alan, like so many "youngests" was along for the ride.

One day at the age of 15, "Crazy" Uncle Har moved out of his house and under the deck of his family home, he couldn't stand sharing his room anymore and this was his answer. Being dirt poor and just fifteen, he had nowhere to go, so he hung up old plastic sheeting to protect him from the elements and gathered whatever he could find to create a space just for himself under the deck. Har is loud and yelly by nature, he is the first one to push you to do something he thought was good for you and the first one to rescue you if you fell on your face...unless you were my mom, he was quite cruel to her, both then and now. Har was the rescuer of the family whereas Linda was the caretaker. My mom was the wild card, always very difficult and yet somehow still Hillis' favorite, this drove Har mad and explains why he has always been so cruel to her.

Hillis was notoriously unreliable, even when not in jail, abandoning his children to be raised by a single mom. He did not supply child support or connection but instead showed up with lavish gifts, like a horse for my mother, to gain favor and would then disappear again.

My grandmother was a proud woman who opted to get a job as a secretary rather than take government aid in a time when jobs for women were hard to come by and divorce was shameful. She worked her ass off to provide for those kids.

Even so, providing for four children on a secretary's wage was nearly impossible.

She once told me a story about a night Hillis came home to visit the kids and pick up a few of his personal items. Times were hard and there wasn't enough food to go around so naturally, she asked him for grocery money.

Hillis opened his wallet and gave her just fourteen dollars. While fourteen dollars may have meant more in 1963 then it does now, it still wasn't much to feed a family of five for a week.

Later that night, while Hillis was in the shower, my grandmother looked inside his wallet where she found five, one-hundred-dollar bills. She didn't take even one but held onto the knowledge that this man was never going to show up for them.

By the time my mother was fifteen she was pregnant with me, I was born just eight days after her sixteenth birthday. From what I understand, my mother's propensity toward mental illness had always been prevalent and that didn't bode well for me or anyone around her. She was difficult at best as a child, having tantrums and creating havoc all around her. My Aunt Linda says', "You never knew which way Kathy was going to go, it was best just to stay out of her way."

My dad was nineteen when I was born. He had a rough upbringing as one of five kids born to abusive parents. They lived in a one-bedroom house in Des Moines and ate government food which meant powdered eggs and canned milk. My dad shared a room with all his siblings and slept on the floor with his two brothers, offering his two sisters the only bed. His father had always been abusive to the boys and also to his mother, but his mom had been kind.

This changed one night just after he turned seven when his mother came into their room while they were sleeping and started kicking him, calling him a piece of shit, and then leaving. The assault lasted just minutes and he was left stunned, lying on the floor sobbing, his only respite gone. His mother continued to do this several nights a week, not touching the rest of the kids but taking her aggression out on him alone. He never knew when it was coming and ultimately became unable to sleep at all.

What makes this more tragic is that none of the other children intervened when certainly they knew what was going on. By the time my dad was fourteen or, so he was able to stand up to his mom and get her to stop but for seven long years, he didn't sleep. Instead, he lay awake trying to position himself against the wall in a way that made it harder for her to get to him, but she always found a way, if she couldn't get space for a kick, she would stomp on him with full force. Unfortunately, as a result he has severe kidney and intestinal damage. This might explain why my dad has no relationships with his family members and has taken on this life mostly alone.

My father became a biker, like a Harley Davidson badass kind of biker by the time he was fifteen, all his friends were and are bikers and that is that, he doesn't stray much outside of that box. My dad laughs as he tells stories of when he used to belong to some of the roughest bike clubs around, running drugs and kicking the shit out of people. He even tells a story of being on the run for his life for three years before he found out the guy who put the hit out on him had been killed.

Chapter Two

The Witness

My first childhood memory is of my father beating and raping my mother, I was two years old. My father had been out of town for a while and when he came back, one of his buddies told him that my mom had been hookin' around town. He came in like a bat out of hell, barely noticing me as he took her by force, squeezing her face between his hand while pushing her into the bedroom with a kind of under the breath, teeth clenched but still shouting anger. The kind of shouting that is sort of reserved but seething with contempt and shame. I want to say it was about three in the afternoon and I was left in our small empty living room wondering why my dad didn't come to hug me as he always did when he came home. I could hear him still shouting at her. His voice louder now that he was in another room, away from me.

"Is it true?" He would ask and then slap her hard across the face.

"Dana, please!" came a cry from my mother.

"Is it true! Are you a fucking whore?" And then another hard slap.

The door to the room was cracked open and I saw my father on top of her squeezing her face and then I saw her face, but not through the door, ***through his eyes***. She was crying, pleading for him to stop and every time she pleaded, he slapped her harder across the face as she flinched. I remember I closed the door but sat there nonetheless, leaning against the wall, listening to the escalation.

When he raped her, I can remember looking around the bedroom at the yellow stained walls, the light coming through the window and the bedspread, avocado green with geometric patterns. I took it all in at two years old, but not from my physical body, instead, it was like I was there in the room experiencing it both as an observer from above, as my father and as my mother. It was terrifying and peaceful all at the same time, I was there to bear witness.

Until about age seven or eight our energy is not entirely our own. The veil between worlds is still thin and the connection between child and parent, especially the mother, is very strong. So, although this was happening to my mother and perpetrated by my father, I felt both the pain and the power while also experiencing some kind of higher knowing that I was more than this experience. There was a peace within the chaos and suffering I was witnessing. I remember truly feeling like I imagine a monk might feel when he watches foolish people creating their own suffering, like I had love for them as though they were my own children.

I can only explain this through what I understand now about spirituality. I trust that God was with me, holding me as I left my body to bear witness to this terrible experience.

Losing control and giving into power and cruelty is an incredible rush. You feel it in the forefront and the upper back of your head. Adrenaline floods your body, and you make your victim *"the other."* There is a sickening pleasure that comes with harming another, even if the motivation held inside is your own suffering.

As a child I felt both the power of dominance and the shame of belittlement as I carried the energy of my father's aggression and the victimization of my mother's experience. The power was easier to take, and the experience almost left me with disgust for my mother.

True to form, by the time I could talk I would directly ask my dad repeatedly about this memory. Every time he picked me up to hang out, the first question out of my mouth was "Why did you hurt mommy?" Every time he answered, "You wouldn't understand, let's go get some ice cream." This was his answer every time until I was 40.

Interestingly, I have never brought this memory up with my mother, even now. I think maybe to spare her further shame and humiliation. I think there must be some embedded instinct to protect her.

This experience stayed active in my consciousness for a long time. Often, a child might disassociate as a way to safely cope and it would come up later in life, but not me, I was all in, trying to understand, at two, at three and every day until I was about forty-five.

This experience was my imprint of family. The peace in my being that I felt while it was unfolding had gone and I was left with these two broken souls trying to navigate life and show up as parents at the tender ages of 18 and 21.

We were desperately poor when I was a child, with both my parents coming from very poor families, there wasn't anyone to ask for help when we needed it. My mother told me a story once about how she used to have to steal my baby food and how she believed the store manager knew but took pity on her as a teenage mom. There were times she said she lived on popcorn for weeks because that is all she could afford.

There wasn't a lot of work for a teenage mom in Des Moines Iowa in the early seventies. My mom tried waitressing, but it just wasn't paying the bills and it was difficult for her to find someone willing to take care of me all the time. Being a prostitute wasn't something my mom did because she wanted to, it was something she did because she felt she had to.

My dad's natural way to deal with any suffering or pain was anger. It was learned long ago when he was a young boy. I imagine his anger was fueled by the hurt and guilt he felt for not helping to take care of his own family. I believe he felt immense shame around that.

Ultimately, in this instance, my father's rage played out in him being her "driver." He would take her to calls and if there was any trouble, he would beat the shit out of whoever was causing it.

There were many nights I was in the backseat as he drove her to calls, again bearing witness. He belittled her every time she was about to get out of the car to meet her John. It was disguised as concern and protection, but it was belittling. I remember this too, it hurt, the kind of hurt that sinks your heart.

My connection to my mother was still quite strong and I believe that some of the experiences she had as a prostitute spilled into me through our bond.

I have no proof that I was abused or molested as a child, but I have feelings, feelings that aren't mine, things imparted on me from those men. I have thoughts that make me uncomfortable that I would never act on but are clear and upsetting shameful thoughts. All my life I was afraid to say such things out loud, but the terrible thoughts became louder until I had to meet them, or they were going to destroy me.

Gratefully, later in life, a Native American Elder and Shaman crossed my path. He was in town for a week seeing clients and I could feel that if I was going to trust anyone with these terrible secrets it was going to be him. I booked the appointment terrified of whatever truth might be uncovered.

Once I sat in his presence, I could feel he held no judgment for me or for anyone. He was there in pure love. It was then that I first said out loud what I had been harboring in my gut and mind for so long. He held me and smiled knowingly before he said, "My love, those are not your thoughts, those thoughts and deeds were put upon you by sick men. It is your duty to meet such ideas in grief and then in love. This is not you, but part of your journey to transform."

Chapter Three

As the Fur Flies

My grandfather, Hillis, was a charismatic man that always had a pipe in his hand and a get rich quick scheme in his back pocket (hence the mail fraud). Sitting in jail gave him plenty of time to think about how his next business endeavor was going to unfold. He had made ties to a mink farmer just before he went to prison and had the idea to sell fur coats in the wealthy mountain towns out west.

Hillis decided to test his idea first, in Steamboat Springs, Colorado. He sent my Aunt Linda out to Steamboat at the tender age of seventeen and helped her set up a storefront before going to jail. She didn't know anything about the fur industry or business in general, but in an effort to build a better future for herself, she went. Hillis, showing his true colors, was such a cheap bastard that he made her live in the backroom of the store rather than pay rent for a separate apartment.

Linda tells the story like this, "There were no sales, not

one and within two months bill collectors started calling. I couldn't pay anything, not the electricity, not the vendors and not the rent!"

"Soon the phone was shut off, which was kind of a relief until this pissed off guy showed up wanting his money or his fur. I didn't know what to do and dad was in jail, so I gave him the fur he said was his and then promptly rented a U-Haul, packed everything up myself and drove back to Iowa."

Hillis had picked the wrong mountain town and an ill-equipped teenager to start his business; but that didn't deter him.

At the same time my aunt was trying to run a fur business in Steamboat, my grandfather had another woman running a store in Palm Springs. The Palm Springs store seemed to hold its own and even turn a profit, though I can't imagine who in the hell is buying fur coats in the desert.

Palm Springs went on to become the place where all the kids traveled through to learn the business before heading to the mountains of Colorado. The Palm Springs store stands today and is run by one of Hillis' ex-wives, a woman named Jeannie.

By the time Hillis got out of jail it was 1974, he had learned that his Steamboat store had failed but the Palm Springs store proved the fur industry was a viable option if he could just find the right demographic.

That's when Aspen came into Hillis' consciousness. It was perfect, Aspen had been a haven for the rich and famous since the 1940's and with the explosion of skiing and disposable income, it had the potential to be a perfect match.

Freak Power

It was the mid 1970's when Hollywood and skiing collided. Considered to be the "Golden Age" of Aspen, this was a time when artists, eccentrics, cowboys, and outlaws all came together and transformed this small mountain town into an alpine bohemia; a secret hideaway for Hollywood-types, musicians, and free spirits of the day. Throughout the 60's, Aspen was a somewhat sleepy mountain town with moderate popularity amongst the rich and famous but in October of 1970, all of that changed when Rolling Stone Magazine printed an article by "local writer" Hunter S. Thompson entitled "***Freak Power in the Rockies - The Battle of Aspen***" and from that point on, the exodus began.

Aspen was a place to get away from it all, a place that didn't gawk at "celebrity" but rather protected and cherished it. A place where stars like Lucille Ball, Goldie Hawn and Kurt Russell blended in with the locals while a young Steve Martin played banjo on the mall. Aspen in its own way became the center of the universe during this time. As Aspen continued to grow in popularity, along with it came money, stature, and fame. As it turned out, this was the perfect place to launch a fur store.

However, after being convicted of a felony, Hillis wasn't going to be able to get any bank loans in his name, he needed help. Hillis was a user, he was only ever in it to make himself money, but he was also charming, authoritative, and manipulative. If he couldn't do something, he would find someone or several someone's that could.

Hillis thought the best idea would be to enlist his four children, that would be four social security numbers and four credit scores that weren't his. With this, more leverage, bigger loans, and ultimately more power. So, when Hillis was released from jail, he convinced them, all of them to go into business with him and move out west.

In classic fashion, those four kids wanted so badly to connect and get approval from their father they jumped at the idea to go into business with him. To be fair, I am not sure everyone really understood that *he* needed them. I think at the time most of them were just excited to be near him, that he wanted them. Everyone except Linda, she had already had firsthand experience of what it was like to work for Hillis, and she was reluctant to do it again...but with little other opportunity, she too was convinced.

What his children saw in him was an opportunity to get out of Iowa and create a better life for themselves. He was promising them ownership in a business and a better life in Aspen. He said he would help them get a place to live and they would start an empire together. This sounded too good to be true, yet every one of those four children packed their bags and left Iowa in search of a better life, several of them without finishing high school.

From this, Hillis of Snowmass Incorporated was born, and in addition to providing social security numbers and signatures, they each got to be an officer of the corporation and a maker of their own destiny. He had promised them it was their business and they believed him. At no point did they realize he was just in it for himself.

Rubbing Ink Off a Bill

I was sitting on the floor of our tiny ground level apartment counting hundreds out of a suitcase. The curtains were closed, and the only light came from the fire, making the purple shag carpet turn from black to lilac. My mom was sitting on the other side of the large suitcase, showing me how to test if the money was real by rubbing ink off the bill onto a piece of paper.

"Do it like this Jessica, ink never dries on real money, so if you can't get any off, it's counterfeit."

I took a bill in my tiny hand and pushed down hard as I smeared it against the plain paper, it left a smudge, so I smoothed it out and set it in a pile in front of me. I was to make stacks of ten while my mother did the same on the other side.

This particular suitcase was from Russian royalty, and they had just bought a full-length Russian Sable and a Chinchilla, so we were counting out something like sixty thousand dollars in cash. One might consider this a pretty intense early math lesson for a 4-year-old, but I definitely learned how to count by tens, hundreds and even thousands earlier than most.

It was not unusual to handle this type of cash in the fur industry. There was plenty of foreign wealth that dealt in cash only and it seemed once the word was out that we were willing to deal with these people and their money, more and more came.

They were all very dramatic, with "darling this" and "darling that," the two cheek kisses and giant diamonds. They would tell their family and friends to only buy from us and it was like there was a code word when you heard that a certain family had sent someone new. We would extend "favors" to some families knowing it would come back ten-fold financially and being that my grandfather was a little crooked, that sat just fine with him.

I was in the store a lot as a kid while my mom worked, I even had my own napping area in the far-left corner under the mink jackets where I could be out of sight. But I was awake more than I slept and got to watch my mom's charisma win over many walks of life.

By this time my mother was twenty, a dyslexic high school dropout that had grown up dirt poor in the Midwest. She could barely read or write and had no worldly knowledge at all, but her "on" personality was charming, confident, and clever. I watched her day after day bend herself into whatever the client needed her to be in order to make a sale, it was remarkable.

As a child, I was enamored with the dark-skinned women from Brazil, Mexico and Greece that were frequently in and out of the store. They were so exotic to me with their accents, so loud, emotional, and seemingly urgent. The way they carried themselves along with long dark hair and beautiful red lips just spoke to how these women totally embraced their beauty. I loved watching them try on fur coats and strut around for each other.

I sort of had this expectation that I too would be a wealthy worldly woman when I grew up. Of course, that couldn't be further from the truth. I don't think I have worn anything but Smartwool in about two months and I haven't owned a pair of heels since I was 19.

At its peak, Hillis of Snowmass Inc. was the largest furrier west of the Mississippi. We had property and fur stores in every major ski town in Colorado as well as a few in California.

The rise from rags to riches took about seven years and was not without consequence.

My mother and grandfather were excellent at remembering each family's details. Everyone's family names, weddings, new babies, and all other necessary information to make their clients feel special. My mother would tell you that she loved it, that it wasn't sales to her, it was the people and I believe that.

Unfortunately, the consequence of all the cash on hand was the accessibility to plenty of the white stuff, yet she found relatively little money for things like furniture or even food. There were now countless days I was alone while my mom slept off her buzz from the night/morning before, unable to get up and help me get to school. Days when I was hungry and all I could find were Hershey bars in otherwise bare cupboards. And days I remember walking half a mile to the town bus at five years old, trying to figure out how to get to school, scared and unsure but trying to find normalcy all the same.

The first time I attempted to get myself to school was a lesson in perseverance. First, I had to pack my lunch; there was little except an old packet of lunch meat and a candy bar, but it was better than nothing, so I put it in a wrinkled old brown bag. Then I had to figure out how to get to the school bus on my own at the right time. I had been paying attention and I thought I knew what to do, but just as I got close to the bus stop, I saw my school bus pulling away, I had missed it.

My heart sank, if I went home, it would be another day alone, I could play in the creek, but even that wasn't what I needed. I decided to try and walk to the town bus that went to Aspen. I had done this a few times before with my mom and thought I knew the landmark to look for to get off the bus, a giant gold eagle on top of a building.

I started walking the half mile along the road to the Snowmass Village bus stop hoping I could figure it all out as I went. I kept my head down as I walked along the shoulder, both hoping to be invisible and seen at the same time. After a thirty-minute walk I found myself on a packed bus headed for Aspen. Everyone around me was an adult and I was scared shitless; *what was I doing, what if I didn't get off at the right bus stop, where would I end up?* My mind was racing.

After what seemed like forever, I could tell by what I saw out the window we were getting close. Now where was that giant eagle? There it is, ok, now how do I tell the driver to stop, oh no, wait what is he doing, he is stopping, there must be a bus stop here, great. Wait, the back door isn't opening, what do I do, I am running out of time.

"*Back Door.* I say, not very loud, I had heard someone say that a few stops before and only hoped the bus driver heard me. I hear the puff of air signaling a change in the brakes…" "*BACK DOOR!* " I say in my loudest five-year-old voice. He still doesn't hear me but a few of the guys I was smushed up against do and shout it louder for me before the driver takes off, "***BACK DOOR!!!*** "

It is a relief when the door to the bus opens and I am able to exit, *now I just have to find that eagle and figure out how to cross the street and get to school.* I notice others are crossing about a block from where I am, so I hurry in that direction to use the same crosswalk, but once I get to the other side of the street I am lost. I see the big eagle and I know that means I am close to my school, but I am still not exactly sure where it is.

My only option was to start walking. I went in the direction of the river knowing the back of my school backed up to it and although I was only two blocks away, it took me some time to find it. When I finally arrived, I was only an hour late.

This single experience fundamentally shaped who I have become. I knew at that moment that I could do anything, and I didn't need to rely on others to help me. It was my ticket to freedom, my understanding that I was capable, and it is how I moved through life well into my thirties; not asking for help and taking care of business mostly on my own. The story that I couldn't trust others to show up for me was imprinted deep in my beliefs.

My unconscious belief system ruled my life, I couldn't trust others and many people let me down. This is what we do, we make ourselves right under the natural law of "Like Attracts Like." If I believed no one was really going to show up for me, they didn't, either because I didn't allow them to or because I chose people unconsciously who would fail me.

I was so relieved to be with other people, kids, teachers, anyone that wasn't snorting white powder up their nose. I was so relieved to be in school learning like I was supposed to, and I took the learning in deeply. I was very serious about it and became the top reader in my class by first grade. But there was something else...I also took in my surroundings, how the room felt, the colors and textures that surrounded me and the way the people around me felt, for some reason that was equally important.

By the time I got home that afternoon on the school bus I had a new confidence, if my mom couldn't take care of me, I knew I could take care of myself, well at least I could get myself to school and for now, that was enough

My mother's thirst for cocaine couldn't be quenched, nor could her desire to go out and live her life in spite of having a young child. One night, she locked me in the fur store with our Doberman Pinscher, Jenny, so she could go out and party. The lock on the door could only be turned with a key from both the outside and the inside, so without the key, I was trapped in the store. I can tell you there is nothing more terrifying than being surrounded by thousands of dead animals and no way out.

It got pretty fucking ugly, pretty fucking fast.

Drugs and money were center stage for as long as I can remember, but there was also a family element that at least for me at the time, was real and true. Having my aunt and uncles around me was wonderful. I got to grow up for a time with my cousins, sharing Sunday dinners and sledding, football games and firewood. For this small window of time, we were one big happy family, even with all the drama and drugs, we were all together and that in itself meant something.

Dancing In Short Lived Freedom

My favorite memory growing up was when our whole family would venture out into the wilderness to cut firewood together, gathering enough wood to serve three households through a cold and snowy Colorado winter. Like most families of the area, we four-wheeled deep into the mountains to gather firewood in the fall when the trees were showing off their spectacular hues of green, yellow, and orange.

The sun was still warm on our skin, but the air was cool and crisp. With each passing breeze the Aspens shed their leaves, dancing in short lived freedom before returning to the earth. Black Birds reflected rainbow light from their feathers as they pierced the stellar blue sky while the Spruce, Fir and Pine offered up their perfume freely, for us to take in like medicine. I loved it here.

The first order of business once we arrived in the wilderness was to scout for fallen trees or trees that were in decline but had not yet fallen. You didn't want green wood because it's hard to burn and would create a lot of smoke, wood needs time to dry out and release all the water it has held in its life. But then again there is a challenge, because trees that have started decomposing are often home to large insect populations, mushrooms, and even small critters, so there is a bit of consideration in finding just the right trees to cut for firewood.

If done correctly, chopping firewood, and thinning out dead trees is considered fire prevention and good forest management. Fire is a natural part of the ecosystem but clearing out some of the fuel prevents the fires from burning too hot and spreading out of control. Colorado is currently experiencing the worst wildfires on record fueled in part by climate change. The rising temperatures allow a pesky little bug called the Pine Beetle to thrive, thus killing huge swaths of forest and in turn offering plenty of dry dead fuel to burn.

Our families would pair off in several groups and have a competition to see who could find the best area with the most cuttable wood. Sometimes we would have to use up to three areas to cut from in order to get enough wood for everyone to make it through winter.

Once our family found the general area of trees they were going to cut, the kids got out of the way. The grown-ups were going to be busy cutting and dragging whole trees through the forest and it was smart to stay clear.

No matter how far away we were, our fun was startled to a pause when we heard the first roar of the chainsaw, moments later the smell of gas would temporarily mask our senses entirely before we heard the thud of a tree hitting the ground.

My cousins and I would always find the nearest creek in search of frogs and snakes while our dogs darted through the woods chasing small critters, never catching them, always returning back panting and happy.

I remember how the light danced on the water, the call of the crow and how the forest was teaming with so much life. But the trees, oh man the trees were my favorite. There was something so sacred to me about the Aspen Tree. Perhaps it is the eyes of the great Aspens, outlined in black on an otherwise silvery white trunk, always watching, like a wise old elder. Or perhaps it is the softness of their bark that is said to be a natural sun block, or the sound of their leaves as the wind moves through them. I can't tell you which of these gifts I fell in love with first, perhaps it was simply love at first sight but whatever the reason, they captured my heart and my imagination and still hold me captivated to this day.

As a child I could feel the vibration of all that life, I remember times when I could see it too...it was then, as a child, that I felt a true connection to the forest and to myself. Much like my experience in the creek, it was in the forest that I felt most at home. In fact, looking back, I can say that the forest brought out the best in everyone.

After about an hour of playing in the woods, we could hear through the loud intermittent buzz of the chainsaw that it was time to head back up to the trucks. The grown-ups would have cut the big trees into small enough pieces for us kids to handle, and we would start stacking them in the various trucks and trailers.

My cousins and I were the log haulers, my Uncle Alan would load each of us up with as much as we could hold, maybe only four or five pieces, then we would carry it to the nearest truck and dump it. My mom was usually the wood stacker, she would grab all the wood we brought and stack it tight, four to six pieces high before moving on to another row. In the background was the ever-present sound of the chainsaw and the hacking of an axe, bringing a tree to its final destiny.

We would do this for hours until all the trucks and trailers were filled. It was hard work but maybe because we were all doing it together, it was fun.

Once all the wood was loaded, my uncles would make sure the tarps were tied down tight to prevent the wood from flying out on the way home. Finally at the end of the day the family would sit down and relax for a bit, the adults cracking open a beer and passing a joint while the kids had a soda and maybe some chips.

Our family would retell the stories of the day that they couldn't talk about over the roar of the chainsaw, like, "Did you see Jenny come up behind me when I was cutting that big fucking tree! I almost skinned her alive!" This was also when my cousins would try to convince their dad to bring home whatever forest creature they had managed to catch. But for me, this was the time I would find a quiet spot against a tree or near a creek and just sit in stillness, feeling, breathing and listening. It was more than listening to the birds sing or the leaves rustling, I was somehow listening in a way that felt like knowing. I felt as though I was part of something bigger, that all this life around me was also somehow inside of me.

I looked forward to this adventure every year and to this day, those experiences up in the mountains are some of the happiest of my life. It was in these woods that my connection with the wilderness was forged. And every time I lose myself (and I have... a lot), every time it is the forest that brings me home to the truth of who I am and what I know in my heart.

In my 20's I learned Aspen Trees were all connected by their roots. That entire groves of Aspens share the same exact DNA, so while you are looking at hundreds or even thousands of trees in a forest, you are often looking at one single enormous living organism. The mountains of Colorado and Utah are home to three of the largest Aspen forests. One tree, for example, has extended itself into 47,000 tree stems, making it the largest living organism in the world.

Following the seven-year drought from 2000-2007, Colorado saw a huge die off& Aspen Trees known as Sudden Aspen Decline or SAD. Drought in combination with excessive nitrogen pollution in the air, soil and water have put incredible stress on our high alpine ecosystem. The resilience of this particular ecosystem is not expected to be favorable. So even if we are able to drastically reduce our nitrogen pollution, the recovery will be slow at best, if at all. This is extremely scary as this is the ecosystem from which our water is sourced. A dying ecosystem will change the quality and quantity of freshwater runoff. This is a very serious reality, and we need to be forward thinking in understanding this challenge, especially given that recovery is not likely.

**When once I wept at the base of these trees in wonder,
I now weep in mourning as they die in mass around me.
We are all in this together, the plants, trees, rivers, animals and oceans.
We are not separate, but a beautiful perfectly woven web of life.
We are not independent of each other but interdependent as one system.
We thrive together or we die together.
-Jess Jacobson**

For the Good of The Company

Our business grew quickly and after only three years in Aspen and Snowmass, my grandfather saw a similar opportunity in the town of Vail. Vail was still in its infancy, but it had proximity to Denver, and it was clear that it was going to grow. Real estate was still cheap, and it was easy to get in on the ground level so to speak and that is exactly what we did. We immediately bought two storefronts and secured a long-term rental space for our factory. We had found in Aspen that having a factory was essential and securing a central space was imperative to the success of the whole operation. The factory allowed us room to monogram coats, make alterations, offer shipping, and eventually get into designing our own line of coats. This factory became the heart of the business.

We left my two uncles to run the stores in Aspen while me, my mom, aunt Linda and my grandfather moved to Vail. At this time, it was decided to separate the Palm Springs stores from the rest of the company. Hillis still kept his ownership in both, but the four siblings no longer had to work with Hillis's ex-wife, a welcomed reprieve.

My grandfather's strategy in each town was to have companion stores, one *"higher-end"* and one *"lower-end,"* capturing the two key demographics of each area. The flagship stores were named Hillis Furs and the stores that followed were called Affinity Furs, only in Vail did we have three stores. My mom wanted something that was unique to her, she wanted the best of the best, both in fur and in location, so they purchased a prominent location on the corner of Bridge Street and Gore Creek Drive. Where once there was a Kentucky Fried Chicken with dirt floors, there now stood my mother's shop, Designer Furs...Vail was changing indeed.

Few people knew the businesses were related and the stores worked together, always for the good of the company. There was competition between the stores, yes, but the main goal was the sale.

We quickly reached a new level of success, finding it difficult to keep coats in stock! My grandfather's answer to this challenge was to manufacture his own coats under the label, Jacques Dumont. We still carried the traditional designers but adding our own label to the racks gave him expansive inventory, a bigger profit margin and a certain stature in the industry. Customers didn't know he was an ex-convict just trying to make a dime, they saw Jacques Dumont and thought he was a French designer, only doing business with us which inevitably, drove the prices up even more.

I could be seen at ten years old carrying fur coats, sometimes four at a time, though they are quite heavy, from one store to another or to and from the factory. The factory was about a block between both main storefronts in Vail. It is sort of astonishing to me that they had a ten-year-old carrying forty thousand dollars' worth of inventory around town by herself, but there I was.

The factory was upstairs above a prominent restaurant, it was completely closed in on three sides but had floor to ceiling windows overlooking Gore Creek on the north side of the building. It was two rooms, the first space you walked into was about 500 square feet, with green carpet and fur coats hanging from the ceiling to the floor creating entire walls of fur! Straight ahead were the cleaning and conditioning machines and in an "L" shape to the left was the shipping area. Along the wall were shelves lined with long boxes and stacks upon stacks of tissue paper for wrapping the coats to be sent out.

Our practice was to let people wear their coat while they were in town and then give it back to us before they left so we could monogram it and do any alterations before mailing it home to them. This way they could enjoy their fur while they were visiting and avoid sales tax all at the same time. Eventually we had to stop this practice, but in our heyday, this was commonplace.

To the right of the factory door was a large rectangular high top sewing table that could seat four. The table was big enough to lay out several full-length coats and properly measure for alterations, but only at our peak did we have four seamstresses.

Cat was our head seamstress. She was a plump no-nonsense woman who always had with her anywhere between two and six yorkies. Cat was an artist at heart, but I also saw in her this desire to be important and for her, I think fur did just that.

The scene around the holidays looked something like this; coats were moving in and out the door at record pace while my grandfather kept watch over his empire standing in the middle of the room packing his pipe. He was slow as he did this, deliberate, all the while listening and watching all that was happening around him.

Mary might be pulling a Silver Fox Jacket down from the rack of "To Do's", checking its ivory-colored tag to see what it needed while Cynthia was taking finished coats from another rack and preparing them for shipment. Cat meanwhile was getting Gary our fur currier organized, filling several garment bags with fur meant for different stores on the other side of the mountains; Crested Butte, Telluride, Aspen and Breckenridge. Some of the fur Gary was moving was replacement inventory while other coats had come from cold storage and were being requested by customers for their visits.

Then the phone would ring, "Hello." My grandfather would listen with his whole body.

"Hillis, hi, it's Judy, I have a customer here looking at the full length Black Glamma on sale for $18,999. He is buying it for his wife as an anniversary gift, he wants to know if we can give him a better price."

"Give me the stock number." He would demand.

"544890" Judy was ready.

"What's the original price?" He was short.

"$25,995" Judy knew the protocol.

"Tell him I'll give it to him for $18,599...and happy anniversary." He hung up before she could reply and struck a match to light his pipe, still looking around to make sure everything was running in order. The phone rang again.

"Hello."

"Hi Hillis, it's Judy again," he knew who it was, he expected a call back, this was all part of the game. "Hillis this lovely man just can't meet that price, can you come down to $17,750?"

"No way Judy, give it to him for $18,250, that's firm, don't call me back, he can pick out a different coat if he can't afford that one." He was curt, put out, but it was all for show.

Every coat was always "on sale," but because almost all our business was in tourism, nobody knew any different. The coat that was marked down from $25K probably only cost about $7,000, no matter what "deal" he was giving his customer, he was making a fortune.

We had an even better margin on the coats we made in house, this is where Clay came in. Clay was the man who brought my grandfather's designs to life. He sat against the back wall to the right where there was a special kind of sewing machine and what looked like an architect's table. Clay didn't like to be bothered, he stayed busy in his corner making coats and smoking cigarettes.

In the opposite corner was a monogram machine. The monogram machine was often operated by whomever my grandfather was dating at the time, some of them would hang around longer than others, but generally, it was some trashy younger woman who thought she could get some money or fur out of dating an older man in the fur industry. It was gross.

Through a doorway was the office, this is where the windows were. It was a smaller separate area that held two desks, one for the bookkeeper, my Aunt Linda and one for my grandfather, though he preferred to be in the factory where all the action was.

We were a very tight group, everyone had to be on the ball, it may have looked like mayhem, but they had it dialed. They were in it for the company, when the company made more money, they made more money or maybe they got approval from my grandfather which for some reason, seemed to matter a good deal.

I think I may have been one of the few people in my grandfather's life to ever call him out on anything, in fact he told my mom when I was about twelve that I could never be part of the company because I wasn't compliant enough. I think that broke her heart a little, but if I had to guess, she didn't want any competition from me anyway.

This was to be expected, the first time I called him out I was five. He had called someone a "nigger" and I immediately stopped what I was doing and interrupted his conversation to tell him he shouldn't use that word. I wasn't well received, but I didn't care, I couldn't help but stand up for what I knew was wrong.

This part of my personality seemed to grow with me, and I often found myself in the position of "truth teller." Throughout my life, I wanted to understand what was being presented to me, be that religion, education, or social norms. I couldn't tolerate what didn't feel right. I pushed again and again asking questions to try and understand, rarely trusting the blanket answer of authority. I have generally looked at conflict as an opportunity for greater understanding and resolution. Though I find I am often alone in that kind of thinking, and it sometimes makes others uncomfortable.

Best Done Bare Assed

My dad and I became estranged sometime around six or seven when my mother started dating my soon to be stepdad, David. When we transitioned to Vail, David came with us, and we all moved in together. David came from a military family, and he was the kind of guy who liked order and respect, which seems fair. That said, he was also the kind of guy that would make me choose the belt he was going to beat me with when I didn't take care of my dishes or mouthed off.

From where David came from, beating a young child with a belt is best done bare assed, you know, just for some extra humiliation. He convinced my mother I needed to be more respectful and had her hitting me with the belt too, but my mom couldn't hit me hard. She was crazy and would put me in harm's way sort of accidentally, but she never wanted to hurt me physically.

I remember a time when David had left three or four huge, red welts across my right upper thigh after whipping me with the belt the night before. I was a thin girl at nine years old and the belt wrapped around my butt to snap on the front of my thigh. The next day at school my fourth-grade teacher, Mr. Treat, caught a glimpse of the welts under my skirt (it hurt too much to wear pants). I can still remember the look of recognition on his face the moment he understood what he was seeing, when his eyes met mine, he almost started crying and then... I almost started crying.

Mr. Treat took me to the side later that day and gave me a hug. "Jessica, are you ok?"

"I guess so." I said, even though I wasn't.

"Is there anything I can do?"

"I don't think so." I didn't want to get in more trouble or upset my mom, so I acted like everything was fine.

I know Mr. Treat spoke to my parents, but at that time it apparently wasn't considered abusive, though I don't know why. The thing is, David whipped me again after that, so I am not totally sure what good talking to him did. Either way, how does anyone whip a child with a belt? Like actually, how can you feel in your body that that is, ok?

Eventually, David and my mom got married and he agreed to adopt me. Thirty years later my dad told me he never signed any paperwork allowing the adoption and that my mom forged all the documents. At this point, she was doing everything she could to turn her back on her out of control life of drugs and sex. Perhaps she could change her nature by settling down with David, a respected businessman, in pursuit of a "normal" life.

I will say I am grateful to David; he did offer a steadiness that I hadn't experienced before. There was always food in the house, and he kept the home warm and orderly. This was a vast and welcome change for me, even if he still beat me with a belt from time to time.

As I got older, David taught me knife skills in the kitchen and basic cooking techniques, he also introduced me to countless foods I had never seen or tasted. This was truly his greatest gift to me, and I honor him for it by passing the knowledge on whenever possible.

Unfortunately, my mother saw David and I growing closer as a threat to both her relationship with me and her relationship with David. During this time, she also actively worked to keep me and my dad apart, something he will never forgive her for. She did all of this while simultaneously telling me that I was creating problems for her and David and that it would be better if I went somewhere else for a while.

Chapter Four

Home

My grandfather's house was not necessarily welcoming, though it is where I felt most at home. From the outside, the house was dark, almost foreboding and only a garage was visible. The home was accessible only by a long dark hallway that gave way to a front door. Because the house was built on a downward sloping hill, you entered on the second floor, upon opening the front door, an expanse of floor to ceiling windows framed a magical Gore Creek and the giant Spruce Trees that grew from its shores, it was breathtaking.

My grandfather had the home decorated in steely light blues and grays, the kitchen was primarily white marble with ugly dark brown cabinets, it was not a particularly warm pallet. He had the largest TV available at the time pressed against one of the windows, partially blocking the incredible view. The bedrooms were all quite small and dark, except the master which had a balcony off the second floor, right over the water. The trees were so close you could reach out and touch them.

The house itself was usually quite cold and I used to lay on the kitchen floor in front of the heating vent under the sink to try and stay warm with little luck.

This is the home where my family gathered for Sunday football and big dinners. It's where my grandfather taught me to play backgammon and cribbage...the loser having to do the dishes (he never lost).

I would bounce in and out of this home well into my late twenties occupying every room at one time or another. It was far more a home to me than my parents' house, our family built it together when we first moved from Aspen. I saw the foundation being poured, the framing going up and the foot thick cement walls reinforced with rebar for the cold storage vault meant to store fur. Somedays I would play in the field next to the construction site all day with my cousins as my family worked on the house. My Uncle Har had an old ice cream truck parked in the middle of the field which made for hours of excellent imaginative play.

I would often take time out from my play to check on the house, poking my nose around to look at the progress. I was fascinated by all that went into building a home. I suppose that is where my interest in architecture and design came from. I felt a connection to this house far more than the people in it and when my family sold it, I mourned.

Red Paint and Spilled Blood

It wasn't until the late eighties and early nineties that we started to see a backlash in the fur industry, you know, red paint and animal rights protests. And I, being who I am, started to pay more attention and ask questions.

While out to lunch one afternoon with my mother and grandfather, I asked my grandfather the young, entitled question that in hindsight was totally out of line. "Grandpa," I said, "How do you feel about making a living off dead animals?"

My grandfather paused, resting his spoon on his bowl of French onion soup, he lifted his chin and looked me right in the eyes before he said, "What are you eating there, isn't that an animal?"

I respond with what I believe is a reasonable argument. "Of course, it is, but it is to eat, to nourish my body, it is not for fashion, we need to eat, we don't need to kill animals for fashion." I gave him a continued diatribe about how now we have the technology to stay warm without killing animals and how I understand that once the only way to keep warm in the winter was with fur (fur coats are insanely warm) but how it was no longer necessary.

He picked up his spoon and continued eating, slowly, deliberately as if considering what I have said. Then his phone rings, his giant cell phone, bigger and maybe heavier than a brick. My grandfather had one of the first cell phones available to the masses because all the "help" called him when customers asked for a better price on a coat. Only he and my mother knew the true cost of the fur, so if the sales staff were going to be able to offer a deal to the customer, they had to call him. If he missed a call, he might miss a sale.

My grandfather finished his call, put the phone down and resumed eating his soup. After one bite he put his spoon back down, wiped his mouth and very calmly and intentionally said to me, "Do you not kill a fly when you see it?"

I didn't really understand but of course my answer was "yes."

Then he says, "So you are deciding what life is valuable and what life is not. That doesn't make sense, you either value all life equally or shut up!"

He then picked up his spoon and kept eating his soup, I had no response. *Shit, was he right?* This really gave me something to think about.

I had my share of dealing with people who were uncomfortable with fur, I mean I was uncomfortable with fur, but I was conditioned. If someone were to ask me how I could stand being in the fur business I would first, make them wrong by asking if they were a vegetarian. If they said no, I would ask what the difference was between farming mink and farming cows. If they were a vegetarian, they were almost certainly wearing a leather belt and or leather shoes or had a leather wallet, so no matter what, they too were using animal carcasses to some degree.

That was a good opener, but still not always convincing, so I would recite the ways in which the whole of the mink was used, bones in the black top, oil in the cosmetics, meat in the dog food. This was a good justification and generally shut people up or at least let me make my point. I wasn't going to let anyone win an argument simply on the emotional disgust of the practice of killing 72 sentient beings and then charging $35,000 for their carcasses.

My grandfather took my mom all over the world to buy fur pelts and check out fashion. They both found themselves well beyond what they might have ever imagined in life. For fifteen years they traveled to Hong Kong and Helsinki to buy pelts. They would then travel to Paris and New York to buy coats and see the latest fashion trends, then up to Canada for more pelts. My grandfather's promises were true, it was nothing short of an empire.

As one might imagine, animosity grew between the four children, and it became clear that my mom was still Hillis' favorite. It was somewhat helpful that Har ran the Aspen stores, so he didn't have to see it, but it was clear she made far more money than everyone else and Hillis never invited Harlan to travel with them, further fueling the feud between the siblings.

Of course, just as the family business was at its peak, my Aunt Linda, the bookkeeper, had had enough. My grandfather was a smart and sick man, he paid her just enough to survive but not really. As the bookkeeper she knew the company could afford to give her a raise but each time she approached him, he said no. This was a very interesting dynamic because technically it wasn't really up to him. The four kids owned the company collectively, he was nowhere on the incorporation documents; he couldn't be. Withholding money was his way of control and he used it to keep her down.

Linda wasn't going to take it anymore, she wanted out and she wanted out fast. This meant she wanted to be bought out, get her percentage of the company, and move back to Iowa. Her disgust for the business and for Hillis was more than just the money, it was his general treatment of everyone around him. Like a dictator focused solely on his own needs, the people (in this case his children), were only as good as they could produce.

Linda tells a story of when my mom was really deep into cocaine, just after we had all moved to Vail. My mom would miss work constantly after being up all-night doing blow and Hillis would get pissed off that she wasn't at the shop selling fur (she was by far the best salesperson). His concern did not lie in the health and wellness of his daughter, but instead in the profits he was missing because she wasn't there. When my Aunt Linda tried to talk to him about getting her treatment (this was the first of many times she was to go to treatment), he refused because he didn't want my mom gone that long, it would affect his bottom line. Linda says this is when she first started to think about leaving.

Hillis refused the idea of my Aunt Linda leaving the company, ignoring her needs and her desires. He was a shrewd and deliberate man and had prepared for this moment, just in case. First, he threatened Linda with jail time if she left and then he laid out the facts that she, as the bookkeeper and an officer of the corporation, was liable for all taxes that went unpaid on the cash sales over the years. He, however, was nowhere on the documents, he couldn't be liable for anything. If she tried to leave, he would get her in trouble, if she tried to force him out, the same trouble awaited, she was trapped.

After consideration, my aunt went to her brothers and sister for help. They would have to agree to buy her out after all. Unfortunately, sides were taken, my aunt and both uncles on one side and my mom and grandfather on the other.

My mom managed to convince Hillis not to bring the whole company down by reporting hundreds of thousands of dollars in cash sales just to hurt Linda, ultimately convincing him that with the others gone, they can build the company as they please, making more money and sharing it only with each other. That thinking is what led to a painful family divorce; a classic "us against them" moment, where no one came out ahead and everyone left traumatized.

After many tears and exhaustive fighting there was finally a settlement for each of the three kids leaving the company. My mom and Hillis kept the business and paid out each person according to some formula based on what they were worth. My Uncle Har getting the largest settlement, then my Aunt Linda and lastly, my Uncle Alan, who didn't do much for the company anyway. I have heard over the years that Hillis offered to buy Alan an airplane (he had been working toward his pilot's license) if he sided with him and my mom, but Alan refused the gesture.

My aunt moved back to Iowa, to the slower pace that felt best to her and with her settlement she put herself through school to become a CPA, a move that has proven to be right for her in the long run. Both my uncles remained in Colorado and my Uncle Har is still bitter to this day about how it all went down, never accepting his ousting and forever in anger and blame toward my mother. Though he still goes out of his way to prove to his dick of a father that he is good enough. It's sad really, the anger has caused him so much pain, but I guess for him it is the best option he knows. My Uncle Alan never really got his footing in the world after the company split and struggles to this day.

My mother and grandfather ran the business together from that point forward. Because my mom took his side, she was demonized by the family, and we had little contact for years after that.

Not only did this break my mom, but it broke me. These were the people I spent every weekend with, either outside in the wilderness or at Sunday dinner. There were no more football potlucks with a full house or cousins to play with, no crazy Uncle Har, no gentle Aunt Linda. Suddenly everyone was gone, and I was the only kid in the family. My brother had just been born but I couldn't play with him, he was still brand new. So, when we watched football, I just sat on the stairs staring into space, I was lonely. Life as I knew it had changed and all that was left was emptiness. I didn't even get to say goodbye, it was like they just vanished. I am not sure if the family considered us kids in the whole mess, but it certainly didn't feel like it. No effort, I recall, was made to keep us in contact.

Chapter Five

Hilltop Ranch for Girls

The summer after the family separation, my parents sent me off to Hilltop Ranch for Girls, just outside of Sweetwater, Colorado. For four weeks I lived in a cabin in the wilderness and much like the experience of gathering firewood in the mountains with my family, this experience impacted me in ways that would shape my life and connection to wild places forever.

Hilltop Ranch was the sister camp to Anderson Camp for Boys, located eleven miles away on a long dusty dirt road. We would sometimes visit the boys camp for dances or competitions such as three-legged races or water balloon fights, but mostly we stuck to our own camp.

The cabins slept ten girls and two counselors, though often we had just one. The counselors were generally great, you know the type, twenty something, in college, fun, cute and kind. All eleven of us would have to share one bathroom equipped with two sinks, two showers and two toilets. Every cabin had a name, though I can't remember for the life of me what they were, we all competed against each other in things like talent shows or who kept their cabin the cleanest.

It took a little while to get used to using an open toilet while others freely came in and out of the bathroom, I don't know if I went poop the first two weeks I was there.

A creek ran through the center of the property feeding a small pond and the mess hall was just over the footbridge that straddled it. Camp meals were signaled by a large triangle dinner bell that rang three times a day, I really like this, there was no uncertainty as to when and where my next meal would come from.

At the end of the meal, we put our scraps into a slop bucket for a pig that no one ever saw and then we would work together to clean the entire mess hall. For some, this task was difficult but for me, it was much easier than being back home.

As you might expect, there were wealthy kids and those whose families stretched and saved to give their kids an opportunity to experience the mountains and rivers of Colorado. Kids at camp were from all over the United States, from big cities out east to small towns in the Midwest. It was clear who was who and I kind of fell into both categories. I was definitely drawn to the kids who wanted the experience more than the kids whose family, like mine, sent them away for their own convenience.

On Sunday mornings, we would hike a mile up a rocky sage field to the top of a mesa overlooking the surrounding mountains, it felt like we were on top of the world. We would all hold hands in a giant circle honoring each other, saying what we had learned, what we were grateful for and someone we wanted to send love to. We didn't worship God up there in the way you might think of in church, but we did sing songs of love and gratitude that had something to do with nature and family. The camp had its own song that I remember loving and singing for years after I went, but try as I might, I cannot remember it now. We would spend about an hour under the hot sun holding hands as everyone took their turn. At the end, we would scream 'YIPPIE!!!'' at the top of our lungs like cowgirls before heading down the mountain to play in the water and get some lunch.

This was my introduction to nature as church, and I am grateful that it stuck.

My church is in the mountains
where Holy water is born.
Flowing down the mountainside
to fill a lake for my baptism.

Red rock and green forest
offer colors deeper than stained glass.
Moose, lion, bear, and bird
make up the congregation.

My church is in the desert,
where far off arches blend into the sunset.

Or in the blessing of snow
as I glide my skis through the trees
quietly contemplating all that I am grateful for.

Chasing rays of Light through the forest
remembering we are all part of this
Oneness.

Camp was heaven for me, every day was lived outside, we only went to our cabin to sleep, shit and shower. In addition to daily activities, we got to participate in several one-day trips as well as a three-day and four-day trip of our choosing over the course of the month. These longer trips were meant to further our experience, sharpen our skills and understanding of our chosen activity. For me, those trips were wilderness immersion therapies, simultaneously opening my mind, strengthening my curiosity, and deepening my heart to the natural world surrounding me.

For my three-day trip I chose an overnight horseback riding trip in the backcountry. Although I had been in the wilderness a fair amount before camp, taking horses into the backcountry where there are no roads and no trace of humans except a tiny foot trail was awesome in the truest sense of the word. The evidence of abundance was everywhere; from massive snow fields to meadows of wildflowers, we encountered bears, who just looked on, not particularly disturbed with our presence and fox families that barked at us all night.

We pitched our tents surrounding the horses to help discourage predators and kept a fire going most of the night. We had to gather our own wood, breaking off in groups of two, just like gathering firewood in the mountains back home. Here in nature, away from distraction, I found peace riding through dense forests of Aspens and Evergreens, across expansive meadows of tall grass and wildflowers flanked by snowfields and craggy outcroppings. This was it; we were in the middle of nowhere and everywhere at the same time. The water we drank came straight off the snowfields we crossed and rather than boiling it or running it through a purifier we drank it outright. We had no concern for getting sick, there was nothing above us but trees, the water was as pure as the snow was white.

Now thirty-six years later, these same headwaters are sick and dying quickly. I have lived on or near a tributary of the Colorado River for 32 years. When you spend that much time near the water, you unconsciously understand it. Temperature, wind, precipitation, and dust all play major roles in our watershed. There are days when I rejoice in abundant snowfall and days when I fear that that same snowfall may be the cause of flooding down valley. With rising global temperatures, the potential for major springtime floods are a concern but the real problems facing the alpine environment today are threefold, diminishing snowpack, widespread death of Aspen Trees and excess nitrogen pollution causing toxic algae blooms in high alpine watersheds.

In the valley where we live, there are multiple tributaries leading to the Colorado River. These tributaries travel for miles feeding high alpine lakes, reservoirs, agriculture, and thousands of people before they meet the Colorado River which continues to serve another 40 million people both down and remarkably, upstream.

In the past two decades we have seen a decline in the health of our forests resulting in degradation of our high alpine waterways. Last summer, many of our lakes were either blooming algae or warming in temperature enough to compromise the insect and fish populations.

It is astounding, I stand at the headwaters for some of the freshest water on our planet, yet by the time it arrives at 8,000 ft, it has already

been compromised, altered, and polluted. That means all the life that the
river serves downstream is also compromised.

Finding Flow

The river we ran for our one-day trips was at the base of Anderson Ranch, so it was easy to get to and from. I had learned a lot already in my limited time on the river, like how to follow the tongue, how a hole could be disguised as a fun rapid and how to paddle a boat with your peers. The raft guide was the person who always directed and steered the boat from the back, but paddling a boat took teamwork and if you didn't listen to your guide, it could get ugly fast. So far, we had rafted pretty easy, class 1 and 2 rapids: not very dangerous but still thrilling for an eleven-year-old.

The rapid I remember most was called "The Washing Machine," not because it spun you like a washer but because someone had dumped an old washer down the bank of the river and there it sat; motionless, rusting, trashing the place.

After rafting the same stretch of river about three times I was starting to crave more. When it came time to choose our four-day trip, it was clear I wanted to go rafting down the Yampa River.

I had never in my life run a river until I came to camp that first summer and I quickly fell in love with it. I couldn't imagine what it would be like camping on the banks of a river for four consecutive nights, but I was game.

On our way to the put-in, our bus broke down, leaving us stranded on the side of the road for five hours. By the time we arrived it was midnight, so we pulled out our sleeping bags and slept on the ground next to the bus, on the banks of the Yampa.

We were all a little groggy the next morning, but the camp counselors and river guides got the boats in the water early and right after a campfire breakfast of pancakes and bacon we jumped in, eager to get on our way.

Each boat had a cooler and several dry bags. All the boats were paddle, meaning we the campers, along with the river, were the power that moved them. It was one river guide to five girls, there were maybe five boats like this. There were also two oar boats that acted as our support, carrying the remainder of the food and gear.

The guides that ran the support boats were the true experts of the river, they knew each rapid before we heard it and would tell us which tongue to follow, they told us to stay to the left or right and what to watch out for. They carried all our coolers and dry bags when the rest of us had to portage (carry) our rafts around a class five rapid, too big and dangerous for us kids to paddle through. I can tell you the portage itself might have been a little too much for us too, but we managed.

When floating on a multi-day river trip you get to see undisturbed wild places, untouched by man. You experience the awe of canyons carved by water, wind, and time with layers of pigment rich in all the colors of the rainbow. Being on the river elevates all your senses and through the nature of the water, you experience excitement, fear, and joy as well as peace, calm and connection.

The first day on the Yampa was so boring, offering a sluggish current at best. I don't know if this was by design, but it really forced us to get to know our rafting partners. There was nowhere to hide and nothing to hide from. There were a lot of bad jokes and showing off but there was also a truth that came forward in each of us. The river was a place where we eventually all found our flow.

Toward the end of day two, we floated through a torrential downpour that lasted about fifteen minutes. With towering sandstone walls on either side of us there was no shoreline to pull over to and seek shelter. There was nothing we could do but sit on the water and float through it.

Our teeth were chattering, and we were shaking with cold by the time the rain stopped. Several of us stood up to grab a layer from our drybags when we came around a big bend in the river and heard a familiar sound up ahead. It was a waterfall, and then another and another still. The narrow canyon had opened, revealing a small valley floor to the south while maintaining a fierce vertical sandstone wall to the north. Here, pouring out of the canyon walls were hundreds of tiny waterfalls, each one cascading into the one below. The rain that had passed through here just minutes ago had collected at the top of the wall only to find its way back to the river through the porous sandstone, creating a sight and sound like no other.

We watched this amazing phenomenon, still wet and cold for about ten minutes before the waterfalls began to slow and eventually stop. As it turned out we would be camping on the shoreline adjacent to this very canyon wall, so we pulled over and set up camp for the night.

As nature would have it, there was some balance to the day as we had to be quite mindful of fire ants and scorpions that night. At least with scorpions there were reasonable tactics to ensure your safety; tap out your shoes before you put them on, keep the tents zipped but just in case, pat down your sleeping bag before you get in, but with fire ants it's a bit trickier. Yes, they had their nests which obviously we avoided but they were aggressive and with all these new people stomping around their neighborhood, they came out to investigate. The ants had no fear of us at all and would go on the attack when we were just sitting in the dirt, it was absolutely insane!

We spent one night on the shore across from the canyon wall, suffering bites and torment from the insects, but at any given moment, I could catch someone looking up at that wall, remembering that magical moment in wonder and gratitude.

By the end of day three we got to experience the confluence of two great tributaries, the Yampa, which is the last free flowing tributary to the Colorado River and the Green. We watched the colder Green River, named aptly for its unmistakable green color, meet the warmer, muddier waters of the Yampa to form one much larger river that would continue to flow downstream before joining the Colorado River in Canyonlands National Park.

Running a river like this is an extraordinary experience, the pure wildness of it is both humbling and exhilarating. Unfortunately, you also see the ugly side of the river, the human side. These are the parts of the river where people have dumped trash, appliances, tires, mattresses, and all manners of crap. You witness the many diversions where man takes the water, harnessing it to serve his own needs, entitled by "water rights," before that same man releases the now contaminated water back into the river. Either unknowingly or uncaringly poisoning the water with herbicide, pesticide and fertilizer creating unintended consequences, resulting in self sabotage for generations to come.

For 6 million years the Colorado River flowed into the Sea of Cortez through an incredible 3,000 sq. mile Delta. Over the last fifty years the river has made it to the ocean only a handful of times but by 1998, the river at the Delta had dried up and no longer met the sea at all.

The Colorado River Delta that supported countless species and carried freshwater nutrients to the salty sea estuary came to an end. The last of the river was harnessed for farming in northern Mexico and all that's left is a dried-up riverbed for 100 miles.

However, in 2014, for the first time in history, an agreement by both the United States and Mexico prioritized the Colorado River for the environment's sake. Both governments worked together in support of getting the river to flow once again. Through the purchase of water shares from local farmers, primarily in Mexico, a small but meaningful "pulse release" was brokered. This pulse release was meant to mimic a spring flood and demonstrated the ecological memory of the Delta, almost immediately life was reborn.

Communities as well as wildlife flocked to the water to drink, dance, and play. Small shrimp like crustaceans immediately sprang to life after waiting years, dormant in the dirt. It was remarkable how quickly life returned. After only eight weeks, the water was gone. By the time the release had made it to the delta, the release point 100 miles upstream was dry.

Both governments and activists see letting this river meet the ocean as an ecological priority and continue to buy shares of water from farmers in order to maintain a minimum pulse flow once a year. And while the volume of water the delta is experiencing is only 1% of historical flow, this tiny respite means life for hundreds of species, a slow restoration for *the estuary but most of all hope. Hope that with the right leadership and support, the Colorado River will once again meet the ocean and bring life back to the Colorado River Delta.*

This is a beautiful example of ecological memory and how, if we lessen our impact even a little, the planet has the wisdom to repair itself. The COVID-19 Pandemic gives us countless examples of this as human retreat gave way for nature to flourish. For the first time in thirty years for example, the smog over Punjab, India has cleared to reveal the stunning peaks of the Himalayas.

God Is Love

I understand now that those early days at the creek and in the forest were my first days in meditation. My need for quiet only grew as I grew. After experiencing Hilltop Ranch and the Divinity I found in nature, I was consciously hooked.

Once home, I no longer had access to nature in the same way and navigating both home life and social life was quite taxing. I found new ways to let go, turning to music as an outlet. Sitting alone listening to music for an hour gave me the space I needed to continue to persevere in honoring myself in a world that not only didn't understand me but also seemed deeply disconnected from itself. I felt different from my family and my friends, I didn't understand the social dynamics of cruelty and conforming to belong, I often felt out of place.

Once the school year started, my mom informed me, I would be taking catechism classes with our neighbor, who was the Pastor of our Lutheran church; I was the appropriate age for indoctrination.

My Catechism classes were more than a Bible study, they were about community, taking care of each other and applying the teachings of God to everyday life. I was open to that and in fact enjoyed learning about God...except that it didn't feel like what Pastor Dan was teaching me had anything to do with who or what I understood God to be.

I could basically get on board with the Ten Commandments, those seemed like a commonsense guide on how to be a good and decent person. I could even embrace the idea that God is omnipotent and omnipresent, that was easy to see when I was in the forest. But the whole idea about fearing God really threw me for a loop.

"If God is love, then why should we fear 'him'?" I said this as less of a question and more of an indignant condescending statement.

I received mostly a blank stare from the Pastor. The truth in his heart couldn't give me a reason to fear God.

Then the teachings around baptism came up and I knew for sure these people were crazy. "God isn't going to send a child to hell because they weren't baptized." I looked him straight in the eye, my heart, and head open, there was no way this guy was going to tell me that and mean it.

"Jessica, these are the laws of God, we must respect them, that is what faith is." he gave me a blanket answer which pissed me off.

"Faith is trust in the light; it is not trusting an omnipotent being is sending a child to burn in hell because water wasn't sprinkled on their head! Think about it!" I was serious in my questioning of Pastor Dan, not because I wanted him to be wrong but because I wanted him to see the obvious error in the teaching. I knew if he just paused for a moment and felt into that teaching on his own, he would know it was bullshit.

I know I challenged him, he would get tired sometimes after we engaged, but at least I engaged, I was committed to understanding. Despite my Lutheran teachings, I knew that all these rules were not made by or for God, they were made by and for man. They were made for control and power but not for God, God was the ruse. There was no way I was going to fear the most loving, whole, and wise Spirit that I understood as God, even at twelve, I knew better.

My understanding of the truth is simple: God is love, we are love, God is both within us and around us, we are not separate from God. The Natural Law of **Cause & Effect** *and* **Like Attracts Like** *serve as the enduring truths through all time and all culture.*

While my pastor taught me how to pray to God, the trees taught me how to listen.

Chapter Six

Poison in the Well

Minturn Middle School was the only middle school for all of Vail, Avon, Edwards, and Minturn. It sat on a campus just outside of town, tucked away in a beautiful valley, surrounded by craggy rock outcroppings atop Evergreen and Aspen covered mountains, there was land as far as the eye could see.

The Eagle River, a tributary to the Colorado runs directly through the town of Minturn and over the last hundred years has been defined by its unusually beautiful orange-and-red-stained river rock. Unfortunately, the very thing that makes the river unique is also what is poisoning all the life within and around it.

The beautifully stained rocks found throughout the river are a result of mine tailings that have been affecting the river and surrounding land as far back as 1913. Toxic metals eventually leached into the towns watershed as evidenced by the ever-present orange water stain in the white porcelain sinks and toilets around town.

From a geographical and socio-economic standpoint, Minturn was an old mining town, situated 1,000 feet below the company mines of Gilman and Redcliff, perched in the mountains above. Years of unregulated zinc mining created millions of gallons of mine tailings, full of toxic heavy metals that were released into the Eagle River and nearby storage ponds. These storage ponds did a poor job containing the waste, allowing toxic sludge to penetrate the groundwater and pollute the soil. These very storage ponds also happened to be my view from the bus window every day when I went to and from school.

In grade six and seven, our class took it upon ourselves to write then-president Ronald Regan to let him know we were being bussed to school alongside toxic ponds of mine tailings. This fit right in with who I was becoming as an environmentalist. By this time, I had spent so much time on the land that I became passionate about protecting it and enraged at the carelessness of man, allowing things like this to happen.

By eighth grade, the President or at least the EPA heard us and sent a crew of folks to test the water, soil, and air. Now, as we were bussed to school, we would see people in white and yellow hazmat suits, hooded and all, taking water, soil, and air samples. In the end, the EPA declared that the children were not at increased health risk, even though poisonous heavy metals were found in everything they tested. These findings eventually led to the same EPA declaring the same land we were being bused through a superfund site, an area where hazardous contamination has been found and requires long term clean up and strict monitoring.

What a crock of shit this was! Are people so afraid of making mistakes and being wrong they would tell us in the same breath that the school children were safe while also declaring the area a superfund site? What the fuck is that?

Middle school is where we start to find ourselves and I was no exception. In addition to becoming an environmentalist I found music. One of the most meaningful parts of middle school for me was band. I began playing flute in fifth grade, once I picked it up, I couldn't put it down. I practiced every day after school, wanting to be the best I could be. I loved the resonance of the flute through my body and became first chair and held it throughout middle and high school.

My favorite part of playing in the band is when both the individual musicians and sections; woodwinds, brass and percussion had figured out their parts and we came together as one to create beautiful music. The way the music moved through me brought me to tears. I was a band geek through and through and spent many days in the band room doing homework or just hanging out with friends, it was my safe space in middle school.

On January 28th, 1986, a time before internet, home computers, cell phones and social media, a time before seeing and knowing everything in an instant was even possible, I gathered in the band room along with about one hundred other kids and teachers to watch the Space Shuttle Challenger Launch from Cape Canaveral. The band room was the biggest room in the school other than the gym and the school had gotten cable wired directly in for this historic event. They rolled out the largest TV they had, front and center, so as many people as possible could watch. For us, the Space Shuttle Challenger was a national treasure soon to be a national accomplishment. Most Americans still had pride in our abilities as a country and the collective excitement around this event was palpable across the country.

We were no exception, each of us leaning forward on the edge of our chairs, dozens of people standing in the back of the room chattering in anticipation. For the first time in history, a regular person, a teacher, was on the shuttle and somehow that really meant something to all of us.

The launch began in earnest when the countdown commenced, then the ensines Fired. Screams of excitement filled the air, we watched with anticipation as the rocket began to lift and then...seventy-three seconds later....an explosion. Everything went quiet and the air seemed thick with dust particles as light shone through the two-story windows; everything slowed down as we looked at each other in disbelief.

For the rest of the day, classes were canceled and teachers, still stunned and grieving themselves, became available to help process the incident. We kept the news feed on in the band room in hopes to glean a greater understanding of what happened, but it almost didn't matter...the crew was gone regardless. The Shuttle explosion was a national tragedy and a collective trauma. At that point in time, we, the collective, were emotionally invested in the success of this flight and when it exploded, it took a piece of us with it. We all needed time to heal.

Mr. Martinez, our woodworking teacher, was particularly good at supporting kids in a hard spot. He would bring kids to the shop room and help us move through our pain by working with wood. He did this for me and a few other kids after the Challenger explosion. Mr. Martinez seemed to see all of us as we were and bring out our best selves, he had a gift.

It was Mr. Martinez who pulled me aside one day in sixth grade (not in shop, he was also an academic teacher, but I can't remember what subject) and told me to hang in there. He told me there was more for me than what I understood now. He told me although I didn't see it, I was a leader and to always remember that when things got tough. I still lean on his words today.

Billy... "The Kid"

Sometime in sixth grade a kid named Billy came to our school. He was kind of a messy kid with big, crooked teeth and crazy uncombed hair, dirty clothes and a jacket that was three sizes too big. Billy, though a little hyper, was a genuinely kind kid. He wasn't well received by most of the other kids and faced some bullying, but I liked Billy ok. He wasn't my best friend, but I didn't mind him, in fact we shared a certain desire for chocolate chip cookies from the school cafeteria and would often run into each other in the lunch line.

One day Billy didn't come to school and then a week had gone by that Billy had been absent. Most of my friends didn't really notice or care, which I would say is appropriate at that age, but one very serious afternoon our teachers gathered us all together to tell us something somber.

Billy had been killed, beaten to death by his parents.

At this age, we didn't really know how to handle it. The

recognition and shame that came over so many faces clear. We all started to understand why his clothes were dirty and perhaps why he tried so hard to connect.

I deeply hope that this experience stuck with others as it has stuck with me over the years and that moving forward, they were more compassionate with outsiders, perhaps more attentive to the tells of someone facing abuse. General bullying stopped for the rest of the year once we learned of the incident, but I don't remember talking about it with anyone, not a teacher or a friend. It is almost like it landed and we all processed it quietly in our own way.

I know many people who talk about how great their high school days were, but for me, it was middle school. It's where I learned to work with wood and play music, it's when I learned compassion and empathy and it's what solidified my desire to fight for our environment. All these things still define me today and I am so grateful for all the experiences that allowed my unfoldment.

Chapter Seven

Hanging by a Thread

While my mom had always enjoyed some level of drugs and alcohol, she dialed it down considerably when she met my adopted father David...or maybe she just hid it better. She still drank but was relatively functional and unless you were paying attention, you wouldn't have noticed. I think the drugs and alcohol were more like self-medication for her anxiety, depression, and whatever other mental illness she carries with her. But when the family and the business broke apart, my mom reacted with what she understood best in a time of hurt, copious amounts of drugs.

I believe it was around this time that Hillis bought my mom a horse for the second time. My mom had always been drawn to horses and Hillis knew this, he had purchased a horse for her once before when she was thirteen. I imagine he did it this time to take her mind off losing her family and give her something to focus on, I think this is when I really lost her. She was lost to herself for quite some time before this, but the horse brought a new dynamic; if she wasn't working, she was riding.

Awareness of her mental illness became unavoidable around this time and while everyone around me spoke horribly about her, no one really understood the magnitude. Even my adopted father David, refused to take me seriously when I spoke to him about her addictions and mental illness.

It seemed as long as everyone was making plenty of money everything was good enough, but it wasn't good enough for me. My family was gone, my mom and David were largely absent, and no one seemed to think twice about any of it.

My Aunt Linda used to hold the role of worrying about my mom and spearheaded her first stint into a drug treatment facility. With Linda gone, that role fell on me, only I was too young to do anything meaningful and my words of concern fell on deaf ears.

I held my breath when my mom cycled into chaos, I heard a lot of, "that's just Kathy," from her staff, David, and Hillis. But I just kept looking around asking," isn't anybody going to do anything?" They weren't, not anymore, they had done things, they had sent her to rehab after rehab. What else was there to do? She hadn't chosen to deal with her mental health or her addiction and that meant there wasn't anything else to do; so, life went on, business as usual.

Standing in our dining room one night, my mother turned on me. "Do you know how hard I work?" Her eyes were seething with anger as she spoke to me like I was her worst enemy.

"Yes, you always work, trust me, I get it." I said this plainly, unemotional, and only partially engaged, but held eye contact, sure if I looked away, she would lunge at me like a wild animal.

"You don't fucking know, David doesn't fucking know, nobody fucking knows!" She screamed while flailing her arms about "Look at all this, is this what you want? Are you fucking happy now?"

"No mom, it's all just too much, I think you could take some time off, maybe we could take a vacation." Again, I am calm and matter of fact.

"Fuck you! Hillis isn't going to let me have a vacation and David isn't going to go anywhere with you! You are the problem aren't you!" She was leaning in now; we were nearly nose to nose.

"Mom, stop it, there isn't anything happening here, this is all you." I am neither leaning in nor leaning back.

"OH YEAH! NOTHINGS GOING ON, WELL WHAT ABOUT DAVID, WHERE IS HE ALL THE TIME? And what about your grandfather, he has a new woman every month, fucking white trash whores. And what about you Jessica, what are you after? You want me to die so you can have all my money!"

"No mom, I want you to calm down, I want you to be happy." She took a step back and pulled her arm back like she might hit me before collapsing into tears on the floor. "Mom, it's ok to be tired, please, just take some time off."

"I don't need any time off Jessica, I am fine, leave me alone." She got up off the floor and stormed away.

My mom was overworked and underappreciated. All she wanted was for someone to see the good job she was doing.

Her "little girl-self" was still looking for approval from her father, approval that came only when he could use it to manipulate her.

That's hard on anybody, but when combined with her mental illness, addiction, and a little bit of power, she was a force to be reckoned with. She became a tyrant at work, blaming others for her own mistakes and demanding unreasonable things from her staff. She was demeaning and condescending, projecting the way she felt inside onto others. The worse she felt about herself, the worse she treated everyone around her.

Laurie, the accountant that replaced my Aunt Linda once asked me, "How do you deal with her Jessica?"

"I don't know." I muttered.

"Is she like this at home?" She asked accusingly.

"She isn't home much, but sometimes I guess."

"Jess, she's fucking crazy, I don't know how you do it." Laurie was shaking her head and rolling her eyes.

Laurie talked to me like I was her peer rather than a twelve-year-old girl watching her mother descend into hell, but Laurie wasn't the only one, it seemed like most of the people that worked for my mom tried to avoid her at all costs. The crazy thing is that they all felt perfectly comfortable talking to me about it. Not one of these adults thought to ask how I was doing, instead they used me like a sounding board to absorb all their complaints about the woman that was supposed to be taking care of me.

Broken Dreams

Through all the ups and downs, Hillis and my mother continued to run the company together for the next ten years. They had consolidated their empire down to four stores, two in Aspen and two in Vail.

With the consolidation of fur stores came expansion into other interests; specifically, the breeding and showing of Quarter Horses. The company sold long held properties that had been purchased for investment in order to finance both the eighty acres my mom lives on now and 136 acres my grandfather bought in Texas in order to bring this next dream to fruition.

After only three years of training my mother placed seventh in the world in Western Pleasure. Western Pleasure is a kind of riding where the horse and the rider look relaxed, but the gait and head positioning of the horse must be exact. It is meant to look like the horse is a pleasure to ride.

This is the world my brother Chad grew up in. She taught him to ride when he was only five and they traveled to horse shows together all summer long. He had to survive his own version of hell with my mom as a seven-year-old trying to care for his drunken mother, sometimes having to carry her back to the horse trailer at night...but that's not my story to tell.

Chapter Eight

Echo Ranch

In the spring of my fourteenth year, my friend, Kelly, and I gained access to a truck that belonged to some rich kid from Vail Mountain School, the only private school at that time. He was bragging about it to Kelly one night at a party and drunkenly told her where it was parked and where to find the keys. He was probably trying to get some action when he told her she could borrow it anytime.

The truck was an old grey Ford, a total beater that I imagine was used to haul stuff around. It was also not likely that it was actually the kid's truck, but his dad's...and why we thought it was ok to take it is beyond me.

We surely weren't supposed to be driving it, neither of us had a license or even a permit but David had taught me how to drive pretty well by the time I was twelve so in my fourteen-year-old mind, I could drive. Kelly and I regularly took this old beat-up truck from an assigned spot in the parking structure and drove around just for fun. Usually, we would take it for a half hour, keeping to the back roads while I tried to teach Kelly how to drive. We were nervous as hell the whole time, but after doing this a handful of times we naturally became bolder and even entitled.

One night we decided to take the truck to a party, which meant we would have it for the night. We were of course, nervous about this, but because we were stupid teenagers and because it was the only way we were going to get to the party, we took it anyway.

Within an hour, everybody was drunk as fuck. Girls were crying in corners and guys were hitting on anything that moved, but everyone was too drunk to know what to do. Remember, we were all fourteen, so this was dumb, inexperienced drunk. I didn't drink then, I found it disgusting after watching my mom for so many years and as I looked around at all this drunkenness, I couldn't understand why the hell people wanted to feel like that anyway.

The drunkenness posed a real problem for a handful of friends as they had no safe way to get home and calling their parents didn't seem to be a wise choice, so there I was, sober, with keys in hand, Jess to the rescue! I could drive all my friends home in the stolen truck! Definitely the right choice.

This also meant that the truck we "borrowed" would be gone much longer than we'd planned. After a brief discussion Kelly and I decided that the noble thing to do was drive everyone home and bring the truck back first thing in the morning. That night we parked the truck on the road outside of Kelly's house and I spent the night with her.

The next morning, we got up early and returned the truck with no fanfare. Of course, we assumed no one had noticed it was gone, but the next time we went to use it, it was gone.

We tried to grab it a couple of times after that, but whoever's truck it was had caught on and we never saw that old grey Ford again.

My parents found out about the party and what I had done about a week after it all happened. I admitted to driving friends home, still thinking I was the hero, but clearly, no matter how good my intentions were, it wasn't enough. I had become a liability and my parents took the opportunity to send me to a group home.

Echo Ranch was a five-bedroom or ten-person co-ed group home in Eagle, Colorado. When I first arrived, an odd New Zealand couple, Sheryl and Serwood were the house parents.

The day after I arrived, Serwood asked me to go to the grocery store with him. Upon parking the car Serwood said, "Why don't you stay in the car, I will just be a minute."

"Uh, ok." I answered a little confused, why bring me only to have me wait in the car? I sat in that old Wagoneer for over an hour, I was hot, bored... and pissed! Finally, Serwood came back with a cart load of groceries. When I saw him, I hopped out of the car with a clear WTF expression on my face.

"You're still here then, good, come help me load these groceries into the back." Serwood started opening the back of the Wagoneer to make room for the groceries.

I did as he asked, keeping my seething anger quiet for all of ten seconds before I blurted out; "What the hell man, why did you leave me in a hot car for so long?"

"I wanted to see if you were a runner." He said calmly while loading bags of food into the back of the car.

"A what?" I had no idea what he was talking about.

"A runner, I wanted to see if you would run away."

"Why would I run away, I don't even understand what you are saying."

"Let's just move forward, you are not a runner and you have demonstrated that I can trust you. Now get in the car, let's go."

Echo Ranch served kids from ages ten to seventeen. For the most part we really looked out for each other like family, all of us were happy just to be out of our homes. We weren't really the bad kids; we were the misunderstood kids. Some of us were abused, others neglected, I am not sure why they took me, maybe I was more troubled than I knew.

We had one kid come through once named Jimmy, he had to have been on the "spectrum," but the spectrum wasn't a thing yet. He did things like put the house cat in the washing machine, I don't think he was trying to be mean, he seemed to just be curious. Jimmy didn't stay long, Sheryl and Serwood quickly realized the extent of care he needed was beyond what they could provide.

Echo Ranch was actually a former working ranch with two dilapidated barns and other outbuildings that sat on a few acres near Eagle, Colorado, thirty minutes from Vail. It was surrounded by hundreds of acres of pastureland full of grazing cattle and sheep as well as a tiny airport that was used at the time for small military training.

When ten kids needed something to do on a hot summer night, we found ourselves utilizing all that land playing *Ghost in The Graveyard* or *Hide and Seek*. It was a lot of fun during summer, in the dark, when the air was warm, and the stars lit up the sky.

The land and outbuildings also worked well for the kids who wanted to raise sheep or pigs for Four H Club as well as for kids who had anger challenges like Dennis.

Dennis was the longest resident of Echo Ranch; he had been there two years by the time I arrived. Dennis had come at the age of fourteen, just like me, but his story was far worse. Dennis was pulled from an abusive household where he watched his mother get beaten trying to protect her children nearly every day. When he was fourteen, he couldn't take it anymore and tried to step in and help her, not fighting but deflecting his dad's punches. Unfortunately, that only made the situation worse and Dennis along with all his siblings and his mother were beaten terribly. The only silver lining is that their injuries sent them to the hospital where they were finally able to get help out of the abusive situation. However, this also meant that Dennis was separated from his mother and siblings, which I know was hard on him.

Understandably, Dennis had anger issues, he could be triggered out of nowhere and had been working hard in counseling to manage his temper, but he couldn't always control it. He had a desperate fear of becoming his father, but his anger was real, and it had to be expressed. Rather than taking it out on anyone, he would go to one of the stalls in the barn where hundreds of old dishes stacked up in the corner sat quietly waiting. Then he would smash them while he screamed and cried and moved through his anger.

In truth, it was an amazing step for Dennis, he was able to recognize his trigger and remove himself from a situation where he might harm someone else. You may not agree with the therapy, but it was an incredible outlet as he learned other coping mechanisms.

The goal of the group home was to allow us to grow in personal responsibility and love for ourselves while moving through whatever trauma we experienced. One way Echo Ranch supported that goal was through both individual and group counseling.

What a gift this was for me, for the first time I felt heard and that what I said really mattered. "Group" had its ups and downs, but we all made an effort to work together. The counselor taught us tools for effective communication and provided a safe space to share with others who had experienced similar life trauma. It is here that we worked out the little annoyances that come up when ten people share one house. This may be one of the first times I actively learned healing techniques such as active listening and mirroring.

The wider community embraced the kids at Echo Ranch and sometimes would offer fun day trips or gifts for us. On one occasion, a community member took us to Rifle Gap where we hung out on his speed boat and took turns being pulled on an innertube.

There was also a young couple who got a bunch of camping gear donated and took us on a three-day backpacking trip in the Holy Cross Wilderness. And then there were folks who donated money every year so we could go shopping for school clothes. It was remarkable to me that people we didn't know wanted to do nice things for us.

My family was generally out for themselves, survival of the fittest if you will.

All in all, I had a lot of great experiences at Echo Ranch and aside from a few assholes at school teasing me for being from "Psycho Ranch," I actually felt much more confident and secure there than I did at home.

After about six months of being there, Echo Ranch was sold to Boys Town, a huge Christian organization with the mission to support children and heal families. Sheryl and Serwood were no longer able to stay because Boys Town put their own trained people in as the house parents.

The transition came not only with new house parents, Mark, and Angela, but with new rules too, they called it a level system. It was a shame because we had all found our rhythm together, if someone had a hard day, we would support them by doing their chore and letting them have down time, but the level system didn't allow for that. They were stringent and there were consequences if you didn't follow them. Forget Dennis being able to go out into the barn and break dishes, that scared the shit out of Mark and Angela, and it was no longer allowed.

The level system worked something like this, there were three levels: red, orange, and green. Each level was associated with certain privileges. If you were on the red level, you wouldn't have any privileges, if you were in orange, you might have phone and TV privileges but not be able to leave the house. If you were in the green zone, you had the most freedom, the ability to go out with friends unattended for example.

Each person started on green, points would be deducted or given based on behavior. If you didn't do your chore or complained about doing your chore, you would get docked points. If you were respectful and did your chore you were given points. Grades, attitude, and other behavior influenced your point value and thus your level of privilege.

It sucked knowing everything we did was being judged or had a point value to it. The level system created a lot of stress in the house.

After Boys Town took over management, there were also fewer opportunities to be enjoyed by community outreach. I am sure liability played a big role, a big corporation can't allow a stranger to take ten kids out on a speedboat, even if the house parents were there. That was a letdown for a lot of the kids who came from poorer families. For some of the kids, Echo Ranch and the community that surrounded it provided experiences they would otherwise never have had.

Simple Pleasures

I had remained on the green level for the first two months the level system was implemented, but one night while I was out with my boyfriend, I smoked grass for the first time. Somehow, perhaps I smelled of it, Mark and Angela knew, and they pulled me into the office as soon as I got home.

"Jess, have you been smoking marijuana?" Angela asked me just as the office door closed.

I paused, "Yes, I just tried it for the first time."

"You know that is against the rules." Her tone became whiney.

"I know, but I am a normal kid, I am just trying things, you know."

"That's no excuse, we are going to have to give you a drug test and you will be responsible for paying for it." She was predictable with her hand on her hip and her head cocked to one side.

"Why do I need a drug test, I just told you I tried it."

"Because that is the protocol when someone is suspected of using drugs."

"But I am not suspected of using drugs, I just told you I did use drugs." This made no sense to me.

"You are having a drug test." Angela was curt, this was her final answer.

"How much does it cost?" I asked defeated.

"Ninety dollars." She answers matter of factly.

"Are you kidding me!" Ninety dollars was two days' work for me at that age, I was not happy!

"No, we will go to the bank in the morning on the way and you will have to make a withdrawal."

"This is ridiculous, what is the point of this when I told you I tried pot?!"

"Well, what if you are doing acid or cocaine, we need to know."

"Oh my God are you serious, you know I am not doing that, give me a fucking break!"

"You're down to red level, thirty day minimum."

This was basically like being grounded.

The next day they took me to the hospital in Glenwood Springs where the drug test would be taken.

The nurse handed me a cup and asked me to wash my hands. I did so while she watched me carefully.

"Ok Jessica, it's time, go ahead." The nurse said kindly.

"Um, are you going to leave?"

"No, it's a drug test." She said puzzled.

"So, you are going to stay here and watch me pee in a cup?" It reminded me of camp.

"Yes, that's how a drug test is done."

"Oh, um, I am not great at this, give me a minute."

Her demeanor softened, it was clear I was new at this, and I wasn't trying to hide anything. "I'll tell you what, I will turn and face the door, is that any better."

"Thank you, um, I guess it's better." I was nervous and uncomfortable. I managed to get some pee out and handed it directly to the nurse.

"What am I going to find in here Jessica?" She was giving me an opportunity to confess as she held up the plastic jar of warm yellow liquid.

"Weed, I smoked weed, it was my first time, I was honest about it, and I don't know why I have to take this test." I was indignant at this point after taking $90 bucks out of my account.

"Are you sure that's all Jessica?" She chides in an all too sweet tone.

"Yes."

"Ok then, we will be in touch with your house parents in twenty-four hours, good luck!" She said the last line very chipper as though I was getting ready to play a team sport.

The next day by ten in the morning the results were in, "Jessica can you join us in the office please."

"Hey Angela, what's up?" I poked my head through the office door.

"Your results from the drug test came back."

"And." I was still totally annoyed.

"And they found trace amounts of THC."

"Yeah, that's what I said would happen. I think you guys should give me my money back." I say with conviction.

"Why?"

"Because I told you what I did, and you still made me pay for that test! That was total BS!"

"Watch it Jess, you will get stuck on red." This is Mark now; he chimes in when he feels like Angela isn't getting her deserved respect.

"Don't threaten me, I am just being a normal kid, you know as well as I do that keeping me on red doesn't help me in any way."

"Jess, this is the protocol, period." Angela was softer, she knew this was bullshit.

"God forbid you make your own decisions Angela; you know I am a good kid."

"You're right Jessica, you are a good kid, but you are out of line right now and I suggest you leave."

Angela and I had grown close, but I was trying to take advantage of that closeness. She was right, I was out of line.

The month on Red Level went by quickly, I had plenty of "siblings" to keep me busy when I couldn't hang out with friends.

I remained at Echo Ranch for a total of a year and a half before the courts determined I was fit to go home and was taking up valuable bed space for someone else in need. I had seen many kids come and go, switched rooms and roommates, and even went through my first breakup here, I would miss it.

I was truly sad to leave, but I too knew it was time. I didn't know what would be waiting for me at home and the uncertainty was unsettling, but I had developed social emotional skills through both individual and group counseling that I hoped would help me make better choices for myself as well as understand my mom better.

Chapter Nine

Flying the Coop

Home life was almost exactly as I remembered it, my parents worked a ton and Chad, my brother had a nanny. The story was the same for me too, if I got a "C" average in school, they pretty much left me alone. It felt to me like they were just biding their time until I left the house again.

One benefit of coming home was the gift of David's old Honda Accord, as long as I maintained my grades and got a job to pay the insurance, it was mine.

I had been working the last two summers while at Echo Ranch and already had some money saved up, so I was able to get the car right away. This allowed me to get a part-time job as a turndown attendant after school at the Hyatt Regency Beaver Creek. I was the person who came by every night to turn down your bed, leave chocolate on your pillow and freshen your towels. It was a perfect after school job, I worked from five to nine, four nights a week.

After about three months of being home, the shit hit the fan. It was Halloween and I wanted to carve pumpkins. As a teenager might do, I made a huge mess and only halfway cleaned it up. This was foolish on my part as I remembered what David did when I was a girl when I didn't put my dish in the dishwasher. I should have known that not cleaning up my pumpkin mess wasn't going to go over well.

Later that night, while upstairs in my room, I heard David yelling about the mess that had been left and what a disaster I was. He then yelled at my mom for everything she must have done wrong to make me this way.

I had had enough; I didn't need to live like this. Indeed, I had left a mess, but for David to be belligerent about it was unnecessary and out of line. I had gone eighteen months without someone telling me I was stupid or worthless, upon hearing it again, I left, fleeing back to my grandfather's house in East Vail.

My grandfather neither welcomed me nor rebuffed me, it was simply understood that I would find an empty room and we would go about our lives. It was the first time in almost two years I didn't have to answer to anybody, and it was wonderful.

Eventually, I was able to get employee housing through my job with the Hyatt Regency Beaver Creek, something that never should have happened given my tender age of 16.

The noise of my family lived in my body as unresolved trauma, but the act of simply getting away was life changing. I didn't consider for a moment what was happening at home with my parents or my brother. I left it all behind, I had to.

I went on working full time at the Hyatt, eventually

dropping out of high school before I got my GED. I had a boyfriend Mike, who was about three years older than me. he was kind, loving and safe. No longer being under the thumb of the group home and getting out of my parents' house for good gave me quiet, it gave me an opportunity to relax and maybe, just maybe, learn to trust again.

I was lucky to have good people around me, people that wanted to host potlucks and go sledding on Thanksgiving. People who loved listening to music in front of the fire and camping in Moab. People who I could explore the wilderness with and who shared my enthusiasm for nature. It was a much-needed breath, but by the time I was eighteen, I knew I wanted more, I didn't want to get stuck or left behind, so I decided to go to college.

Continuing Education?

My mother had always told me that she would pay for college, within reason. When I reached out to her to share my intentions, without hesitation she confirmed her commitment. She would pay tuition and books, but the cost of living would fall on me. I found that to be more than generous and began looking at schools.

The paperwork was overwhelming and my shame for not finishing high school was almost suffocating, but true to my character I persevered. Because I scored well on my GED, I had options, but not a lot, it was going to have to be a state school.

The process of exploring colleges brought my mom and I closer, she was quite proud of me; remember she dropped out of high school by the time she was fifteen. We explored the campuses of University of Colorado Boulder, Colorado State University in Fort Collins, and The University of Northern Colorado in Greeley, enjoying the traditional college tours. Our eyes were wide as we witnessed the inner workings of a bustling almost independent community, neither of us having experienced anything like it. It was soon determined that CU was too big and not my vibe and while I did like CSU, I wasn't in love with Fort Collins. For whatever reason I was drawn to UNC, and it was clear after that visit that I would go there.

The unique gifts and challenges of dorm life continued to inform my existing feelings on God, drugs, and alcohol. As it turned out, my college roommate, Amanda, was a true hearted Christian, meaning she shared the love and light in her heart as a living example of God's love. She was less "the judgy" religious person and more the "help lift others up" kind of religious person. We had many conversations throughout our time together that mirrored the conversations I had with my Pastor. Amanda wasn't able to answer my questions any better than Pastor Dan and even though my goal was not only to understand her but for her to understand me, there were some hard nights as we tried to sift through it all together.

In the end we agreed our understanding of God was different but still shared great love and respect for each other. She was committed to living her life according to the bible and I simply couldn't comply. Regardless, her light inspired me, she was an incredible human being and I acknowledged I had room to grow. It was time to do more digging into myself to find my own light...at least unconsciously.

I know that college for many means partying, but so far in my life, partying showed me the worst in people, I still didn't want any part of it. Watching freshman "rush" for a sorority in a drunken stupor was almost worse than watching fourteen-year-old drunk girls. At least at fourteen you have no idea what you are doing but by eighteen and nineteen, you might have a little more self-respect. No such luck and time after time girls came back to the dorm puking and crying. I never could figure out why that was appealing.

Even though I loved the general experience of college, it was clear pretty early on that sitting in lecture halls of 500 people was not my kind of learning. I wanted to be engaged, interactive and participatory, something that freshman year at a state university did not offer in any way. Even the classes I took at my local community college before I went to university were more interesting than what I was(n't) learning here. I did however meet several people that were pivotal in my continuing development including my friends Autumn and Courtney.

Autumn and Courtney were my hippy friends, the people I found at school that were most like me or of my tribe. I didn't know I could have a tribe, yet there we were, it's like we had known each other forever. We had similar values, standing up for clean air and water, free love, and tree hugging. It was the first time I truly identified as a "hippy" and understood what that meant as a whole and for myself. It was yet another "*ah-ha*" moment into understanding my true nature.

As the school year came to an end, I made plans to head east, first stopping by the Chicago suburbs to drop Autumn off at her home before continuing to New York City. If I made it to New York, I had a place to stay on 5th avenue; not that I knew then or now what that means, but it sounded cool at the time. After dipping my toe in the bigger world at the university, I was curious and in search of what else might be waiting for me.

Chapter Ten

Chicago Part 1, The Lesbian Years

My introduction to Chicago began when I dropped Autumn off at her home in the Chicago suburbs and she introduced me to her friend Cathleen. I couldn't take my eyes off her and I was drawn to her like I had never been drawn to anyone.

The second night we were there, Cathleen offered to take me out with her to a bar in Chicago, I was only 19 at the time, but she said it wouldn't be a problem.

We arrived at *Paris Dance* around 11p.m. It was in a seedy neighborhood in the city and the big black parking attendant made sure we had a safe place to park, I guess Cathleen was a VIP.

We could hear the music pumping from outside as we walked toward the entrance. The bar had two distinct sides; to the left was the big bar with plenty of seating and two electronic dart boards while to the right was the dance floor with a small bar and a few high-top tables.

Right away someone spots Cathleen. "Hey Cathleen, over here," a young woman with long dark hair waved us over.

We head to the left and sit near one of the dart boards, joining three other women: Michelle, Misty, and Danielle. The three of them are smoking and Cathleen joins them, lighting up a Marlboro Light.

Ugh, I thought...I fucking hate smoking!

"This is Jess, she is passing through from Colorado." Cathleen introduces me.

"Hey Jess." came three voices almost in unison.

"Hi guys." I was feeling shy.

"It's her first time in a lesbian bar, give her a minute." Cathleen is being pragmatic though it sounded a bit rude. They all looked at each other with glee in their eyes.

"What do you think, Jess?" asked Michelle.

"It's cool not to worry about guys hitting on me all night, I feel relaxed actually."

"Don't you worry, you will have some ladies hitting on you in no time."

"Jess isn't gay." Cathleen was blunt.

"Well, I am not opposed to it." I reply a little defensive.

"Oh, you're not gay, why did you want to come out?" There was a sense of withdrawal from Michelle.

"I don't know, to see what it was like, to have an experience." I saw from their reaction this might have been a little offensive, though I didn't mean it to be.

"Do you want a drink?" Misty was trying to break the subtle tension that had crept in.

"Just a Pepsi please." I still didn't drink much.

"Sure thing sister."

"I think I am going to go dance, does anyone want to come?" The music was making me move, I had to get out there.

"No way." they all replied almost in unison.

I made my way through the crowd, finding the raised dance floor on the other side of the bar. Nervously I stepped up onto the dance stage, there were women dancing all around me and I couldn't help but let go. Suddenly, I felt completely uninhibited, and I danced more freely than I had ever danced before, I felt like I was home.

I got hit on a bit and even kissed a woman that night, Michelle, Misty, and Danielle giggled at my inexperience, but warmed up to me easily after that first bit of tension.

The bar started to clear out around 1 a.m. when a big rainstorm moved in. Before I knew it, we were dancing in the parking lot in the rain, jumping in puddles and laughing our asses off. It was a little like a *"Friends"* moment had it existed back then.

Cathleen had stayed warm and dry in the bar, watching us out the window. When the time came to go home Cathleen gave me some shit. "It looks like you had fun?"

"Oh, it was great!" I am still a little out of breath and soaking wet.

"You still straight then?" She asks dryly.

"I don't know, it just felt so easy to not have to worry about getting hit on."

"But you did get hit on."

"I know, but it was different, I didn't mind it, I didn't have to have my guard up."

Being with a woman had never occurred to me and I genuinely loved my boyfriend Mike, but my attraction to Cathleen was instant and all-consuming. That combined with the freedom I felt that night, opened me up to a life with new possibilities.

Cathleen was going to school at The University of Chicago and needed another roommate for her apartment in Hyde Park. I had no real reason to continue to New York, I was just traveling to travel, so I decided to stay in Chicago and move in with Cathleen.

Cathleen was a simple girl, short brown hair, maybe 5'5, average weight with brown eyes framed by black wire rimmed glasses. She dressed like a typical lesbian of the time in jeans, a simple t-shirt with a chain on her pants holding her keys. She also played guitar, both six and twelve string.

I have found that through the years, the musicians turn me on the most and I have enjoyed a few.

Living with Cathleen exposed me to a whole new world of intellectuals, diversity, and food. We attended gatherings with University of Chicago students using their brains for something bigger than themselves, a stark contrast to my experience at the University of Northern Colorado where I attended school.

At UNC I listened to girls, singing degrading songs and getting drunk but at U of C, conversations would range from religious freedoms and philosophy to world governments. I sat in awe most of those early days, just soaking it in. It made me realize how limited my upbringing had been and how much I really had to learn.

There was also an artistic quality to these young adults that I hadn't experienced at home or at UNC, they exuded a confidence and authenticity I had not seen before. Young people were freely expressing themselves through their clothes, hair, tattoos, and piercings. Everyone felt full of life, creativity, intelligence, and passion for what they believed in, so much so that I was moved to reflect on my own life and once again... explore what moved me.

For now, what was moving me was the amazing new food I was discovering in Hyde Park, and I often found myself indulging in things I had never heard of, prepared in a dish I could hardly pronounce. My first such experience was at a laundromat with our roommate Sarwat. We were doing laundry when we noticed there was a falafel joint attached to the laundromat. Sarwat was psyched and quickly went to grab some food.

"Do you want anything?" Sarwat asked.

"I don't know, I don't even know how to pronounce these things, let alone what they are."

"Oh my God, have you ***never*** had falafel?" Her eyes were wide in disbelief.

"No."

"Baba ghanoush?"

"Baba what? "No."

"Ok, I am getting you some falafel, do you want it with or without tahini?"

"I have no idea."

"Ok then, with." Sarwat soon handed me a yellow plastic basket filled with a pita stuffed with what looked a bit like meatballs, cucumber, tomato, onion, greens and some white course sauce, tahini.

"Oh my God this is the best falafel I have ever had; you have to take a bite!"

Reluctantly, I did, it was like nothing I had ever experienced. The flavor was fresh but spicey and those balls that I thought looked like meat were actually more like fried dumplings with a soft flavorful center. It was my new favorite food, and I knew where I was going to do laundry from now on. I had never had a chickpea in my life, I still had no idea what tahini was, but I ate it up like a stoned hippy at a Dead show.

Sarwat was one of my favorite people that summer. She was from Bangladesh and had received a scholarship to The University of Chicago. Her father was a doctor in Bangladesh, but they couldn't afford to travel to Chicago with her, so she was on her own. Sarwat was a beautiful long-haired hippy with a wide toothy smile who dressed almost always in long purple dresses. She brought a groundedness to me which was very helpful given my insane crush on Cathleen.

Mellow Yellow

I got a waitressing job at a little cafe called Mellow Yellow, about four blocks away from the apartment I shared with Cathleen and Sarwat in Hyde Park. I wouldn't have thought that walking four blocks to and from work would have been so eventful, however three distinct incidents changed that assumption.

Walking home from work on my second day I got flashed by a twenty something, I laughed out loud and asked him what he was hoping to get out of it. Since then, I have been told that was the exact wrong thing to do (I learned during my time in Chicago that people think ignoring things is the best way to go about a day) but perhaps because he didn't expect it, he too didn't know how to respond and quickly covered up and rushed past me.

On another day as I was walking to work, a homeless man fell over and hit his head hard on the sidewalk. Naturally I stopped and tried to help, but the people all around us just stepped over him, more annoyed he was in the way than concerned he was hurt. He was clearly unconscious, and blood was seeping out of the back of his skull, so I asked a woman in the store that he had fallen in front of to call 911. She let out a huff like I was putting her out before going back inside to dial.

"What are you doing girl, don't touch him!" came a voice from a big black woman standing over us.

"What do you mean, he is hurt!"

"That's his own doing, you leave him alone girl, you gonna get sick if you touch that man."

Not touching him was the clear consensus, yet I kneeled next to him, touching his shoulder, wondering how I could help. Still, people continued to step over him, muttering things to themselves, just loud enough for me to hear.

"Goddamn drunk!"

"Get him off the fucking sidewalk!"

It was clear his proximity on the sidewalk was causing the most frustration, he was in the way. When I stood up in recognition that I had to get to work I noticed how some folks had no problem trying to nudge him over, out of their way with their feet.

"Hey, wait, don't do that, Oh My God, what are you doing?!" I was horrified.

I couldn't stay as I had to get to work, but I knew the woman in the storefront had called 911 and there was nothing more I could do. I walked away from that incident, dumbfounded.

I had experienced nothing that could have prepared me for life in Hyde Park and I am grateful to have been exposed to it with no prejudgments or fears, I was just wide-eyed, taking it all in. This made me a good mark for just about everybody, homeless, pervs and scammers alike. I wasn't afraid to engage, but I learned, maybe a little slowly, that boundaries were necessary.

I had given food to a young mother the first week I was at Mellow Yellow without much thought other than wanting to help, but that woman began to watch for me and would approach me every day asking for a handout. She quickly became pushy when I was unable or unwilling to continue to support her and her three kids.

"You don't know what it's like out here for people like me!" She screamed in desperation.

"You're right, I don't, I am so sorry you are struggling, are there not services for you?"

"I don't need no fucking services, give me some fucking money, I need to feed my kids!"

"Listen, I need to take care of myself, I can't keep giving you money, I could maybe bring you some food once a week or something, but I can't keep giving you money."

"YOU'RE A FUCKING HONKY BITCH, I THOUGHT YOU WERE DIFFERENT, I THOUGHT YOU FUCKING CARED!"

I stood there stunned for a moment, "I do care, but I can't take care of you and your family, I AM 19, just trying to make it myself. I think you should leave me alone."

"OH SURE, NOW YOU WANT ME TO LEAVE YOU ALONE, NO FUCKING WAY, I AM GOING TO GET MY MONEY BITCH, HOW MUCH YOU GOT ON YOU NOW?" She stepped toward me with her hands out, going for my pockets.

"WHAT THE FUCK? GET AWAY FROM ME, I AM NEVER GIVING YOU ONE MORE DIME, YOU MANAGE YOUR OWN SHIT! GET AWAY, GET AWAY!" I stepped back several steps but didn't dare turn my back on her. I kept my eyes locked with hers until she turned around and walked away. I still stood there stunned for a few minutes trying to shake the experience. It brought back memories of my mother coming at me like that and my adrenaline was pumping.

The next day when I was leaving work, she approached me again, perhaps testing my commitment.

"Hey there girly, how you doing today?"

 Shit it was her again. "Look, I told you to stay away from me, I don't have anything for you."

"You still upset about yesterday girl, that ain't no thing, don't worry about it. You got a little something for me today?"

"NO, I DON'T, I TOLD YOU TO STAY AWAY FROM

ME AND I MEAN IT!" This time I turned and walked away while she called me every name in the book and even a few names I had never heard, I was scared shitless.

Lay of the Land

Chicago is a city made up of neighborhoods and small communities often defined by ethnicity or culture; there is Ukrainian Village, Boys Town, Andersonville, Bucktown, Logan Square and Chinatown, just to name a few of the area's I frequented. And while all these areas served a specific population, they had one thing in common, giant old trees with limbs that spilled over the roads creating an emerald canopy of shade in the sweltering summer heat. A welcome reminder of nature's grandeur in an otherwise concrete jungle.

While most of the neighborhoods had a clear vibe and served a specific community, Hyde Park, where I first experienced the city, was different. Hyde Park has a very unusual demographic as it spans every socioeconomic demographic and ethnicity imaginable. It was home to both President Obama and the poor University of Chicago students. There is profound homelessness mixed with roots in black activism, Muslims, Chinese and everything in between. Coming from a very "white" Colorado, my mind was blown, I loved it.

The city of Chicago is built along the southwestern shore of Lake Michigan, an incredible lake that sometimes feels more like an ocean, with sandy beaches, waves, and water as far as the eye can see. The city has done a wonderful job creating and maintaining lakefront green space complete with exercise trails and dog parks. The wide-open space to the east was a welcome respite to the millions of people crowded together to the west. The lake offered a natural boundary from chaos to peace and back again.

When I first moved to Chicago, I was invited to meet friends at the Belmont Rocks, a huge "green space" along the lakefront. Where I come from, if you are meeting someone at the "rocks" it means you are going climbing, so I brought my climbing shoes. Once I arrived at our picnic spot, my friend's kind of giggled at me and told me clearly that rock climbing wasn't going to be an option, but I had to see for myself, maybe I could do some light bouldering. Of course, once I walked the fifty yards to the lake, I saw the "rocks" were just rectangular concrete slabs meant to reinforce the shoreline. Now, I understood why my friends were laughing at me.

Cathleen continued to be my world for a solid six months, she had a girlfriend, but I acted like her sidekick. We would go out together almost every night, driving her jeep with the top off down Lake Shore Drive and pull into our favorite bar up north while blasting Salt n' Pepper. We thought we were so cool. Perhaps we were, they always saved a parking spot for us, and everyone knew our names. It was a little like "Cheers" but with lesbians, we were everyone's favorite little baby dykes.

Even though I knew Cathleen wasn't interested in me romantically, I continued to be obsessively drawn to her. I made myself available for whatever she wanted to do, whenever she wanted to do it. I would even cancel plans with friends if she wanted to hang out, all the while pretending I wasn't interested, never telling her my feelings, it was brutal.

Although Cathleen was the only thing I could think about, I was young and horny, I had no idea what it meant to be in a lesbian relationship or what sex would be like. In an ever-twisted game of showing Cathleen we were just friends, I started to branch out and find a lady of my own.

The transition for me from straight to lesbian was not a big deal, it felt fluid and natural to be attracted to a woman.

The first girl I went on a date with took me to an Ethiopian Restaurant on Clark Street where we ate with our hands and drank wine made of sweet nectar. I was giddy with adventure. Her name was Jenna, and she was about six years older than me. She knew what she was doing and after a wildly erotic meal, I took her home as my first lesbian lover.

Kissing a woman was just softer, sweeter, more sensual somehow. I loved the way our bodies fit together with entangled legs and writhing pelvises. Our breath was hot on an even hotter summer night and the sticky night air added to our already dripping bodies. I learned that night that a woman knows what to do for a woman more than any man I have ever been with, even to this day.

Apparently, that same night, Cathleen had a fight with her girlfriend and left her keys at her girlfriend's house. She rang the bell and yelled in the window, but we were so wrapped up in each other we didn't hear her over the sound of our own moans. Cathleen had to go back to her girlfriends with her tail between her legs and I caught a ton of shit for it the next day, but it was worth it...very, very worth it. I was still drawn to Cathleen, but I had experienced something powerful all on my own and all I could do was smile, my body still alive from the night before.

Jenna didn't turn out to be more than a girl I dated a few

times, but she did show me magic in bed and prepared me for girlfriends to come.

Within four months I was convinced I was a lesbian through-and-through and made what I perceived as the necessary adjustments. The biggest change was that I cut off my long, beautiful blond hair. I was still a hippy at heart but changed out my long colorful skirts for Levi's 501's and put my keys on a carabiner, which I already had from rock climbing.

With Cathleen's help, I made a coming-out video for my mom and David. I didn't really need them to approve, and it didn't occur to me they wouldn't; I was simply young and excited about my new life and wanted to share it.

"Hey mom, did you get the video I sent?"

"Yes."

"Well, what do you think?"

"I think it was inappropriate to ask the whole family to watch it, it was not appropriate for Chad." Chad, my brother, was maybe eight years old at the time.

"Oh, why?"

"Seriously Jessica, you must know this is a phase, you had a serious boyfriend for three years."

"I know, it's just that this feels really good, are you mad?" In the background I hear David trying to get the phone from my mom.

"Jessica, look, this kind of shit is not welcome, don't you dare set foot in this house until you get your head on straight! I will not have my son exposed to people like you." David had taken the phone from my mom; he was being an asshole.

"What, David, I am not going to make Chad gay just by being around him." I was pissed.

"Do not call here again, we are done do you hear me, done!" Then the line went dead.

My naivete was extraordinary on many levels, much like not being exposed to diversity in ethnicity, I had no idea the challenges gays and lesbians faced in the world. It was the early 1990's and Ellen hadn't come out yet, in fact she didn't even have a TV show yet. This was the beginning of my education on the struggles in the gay and lesbian community.

Once the University of Chicago started their fall session, I had to move out as new roommates attending school moved in. I was lucky to find a place with Misty and Danielle, two of the women I met the first night I was in town.

This is when I would say my life really changed. These women saw so much in me that I didn't see in myself. They were friends like I had never had, loyal and honest even when it was hard. They cared for me and each other like family. I tried to push them away out of defense and fear that I would get hurt, but they called me out right away. These are the women in my life that taught me about love in friendship.

Before meeting these women, I had friendships but generally kept them surface deep. I shared deep experiences with people, like in band class or with Amanda, my college roommate, but I stayed somewhat protected. Upon reflection, I recognize that losing my family when I was young really hurt me and I was afraid to get close to people.

One night, about a week before Christmas, Danielle was musing about the future, "Do you think we will all still be celebrating Christmas together in ten years?"

"What, no, we won't even know each other in ten years." I say flippantly.

Danielle was rocked, "Then why the fuck are we building a friendship now Jess? Do you know how hurtful that kind of comment is?" she started to cry, I had struck a chord.

Holly shit, I wasn't expecting that, "What? I don't know, I have never had friends last ten years, I don't know."

After a long drag on her Marlboro Light Danielle replies "Well, I love you, you should think about that."

I was stunned. Danielle was so honest with me and the three women sitting in the living room with us were all consoling her and looking at me. "Jess, come on, do you mean that?"

I did. No one had ever been present in my life like that before, I didn't know how to handle it. I didn't even understand why it mattered.

It mattered because we all came out in the eighties and early nineties when there wasn't much of a safe space and acceptance was not expected. We were tight, not only because we enjoyed each other's company but because many of us became family, as some of our families disowned us when we came out. We were tight because there was safety in numbers and because few people understood the hardship we experienced in our everyday life, just because we were gay. I did not understand that as I sat there in the living room making my friend cry, but I would soon.

I never really had good friends in high school, partly because of my life circumstances of moving around a lot and partly because high schoolers tended to be dumbasses. I saw people be cruel behind someone's back and then fake nice to their face and I didn't want any part of that. The few good friends I did have turned on me for reasons I still don't understand and therefore I was weary of getting attached.

The women I met in Chicago were nothing like those girls in high school and they weren't going to engage in my insecurity with so much love on the line. Instead, they called my bluff and loved me through my learning, they became my family.

When Christmas came around a week later, one of my gifts was wrapped in a brown paper bag with a drawing on the front of a skier on a mountain. The writing said something to the effect of *Jess's self-help group through love and nature.* They saw me as a healer, even though I don't think I demonstrated any of those qualities then. It took my breath away and it was the first time I realized what I was here to do. I didn't really know what that meant or looked like, but I knew I was here to help others.

I cried because I had been seen, really truly seen for the first time in my life and there was no going back. The peace and relief in my heart felt familiar, like the peace and ease I felt as a child sitting in the forest.

I stayed in Chicago learning what it meant to be gay, when to be careful, how to deal with gay bashing etc. I explored ethnic food of all varieties and indulged regularly in dancing my ass off in Chicago's many great gay dance bars. I experienced my first Pride Parade, learned what a drag queen was and explored S&M. I ate at all night diners at 3am and talked about all the problems of the world and how to solve them while at the same time sucking hard on a cigarette.

I was doing all the stuff you do when you leave your parent's house and explore life on your own, I fucking loved it!

The only thing I didn't love about my new life was smoking, I hated smoking. My mom smoked and I always thought it was gross, but everyone I knew smoked in Chicago, I was getting nowhere trying to convince them to stop. Then one day while I was getting gas, I decided to buy a pack of Marlboro Lights, they were disgusting. I hated the way they tasted, they left yellow stains on my fingers and generally I just wanted to puke...so naturally, I had another. I remember asking myself what I was doing and saying out loud, "if you can't beat 'em, join 'em!" I managed to pick up a two pack a day habit in no time.

My first real lesbian relationship was with a girl I met early on when I was still hanging out with Cathleen; her name was Rhonda. Jesus, she was an incredible lover, we were both very young and similarly traumatized, we bonded over our shared experiences. In classic lesbian style, within a month I moved out of the place with my ladies and moved in with Rhonda. We lived together for about three months before things went south.

Given our similar trauma, we decided to try cocaine together in search of why our mothers chose the drug over us. We would do a few lines, then pace around our basement apartment in Boys Town sharing our childhood stories. In retrospect it was pretty weird, but in a way, we were trying to heal and make sense of where we came from.

I fell into cocaine hard and fast, within a month it took me down. I lost my job and alienated my friends, but I didn't care, I just wanted to do my drugs and dance my ass off with Rhonda.

One morning in August, very near my twentieth birthday, I came out of my zombie cocaine daze. It was six in the morning, I had been awake all-night walking around Boys Town, Rhonda had passed out and I didn't really know what to do or where to go. I was pale as a ghost and weighed about 99lbs. I was pretty skinny to start with for someone who is 5'7" at 115lbs but dropping down to 99lbs made me look sickly.

That morning I realized how lonely I felt, I had pushed away my group of girls...my family, so I could do a bunch of blow with my girlfriend. I felt empty and alone, I had had enough and that was the last time I ever touched cocaine.

Rhonda and I broke up soon after and my ladies opened their arms and gave me a place to live until I could figure things out. They never stopped believing in me, but they also gave me some much-needed tough love.

The Imprint

At the same time that I left Hyde Park I left my waitressing job at Mellow Yellow, it would have been a bitch of a commute for a waitressing job. I had worked since I was fourteen and had been paying my way since I was sixteen. I was no stranger to work, but somehow, finding work in the city was challenging for me.

I didn't get a job right away and as time passed, I almost felt paralyzed, like I didn't know how or where to look. Certainly, there were jobs to be had, but the city was so big and overwhelming, I didn't know where to start.

On a particularly cold and rainy November afternoon I sat in my living room chain smoking and staring at the TV. I was worried about what I was going to do for money when I noticed *Donahue* was interviewing sex workers. Each guest told their story of rags to riches and how they didn't have to work much. Of course, some of the women were flamboyant drama queens but there were also a few "escorts" that seemed like good respectable people.

I left the house before the episode was over in search of a *Reader*, our local paper, to see if there were any ads for escorts. It was an out of body experience, like I wasn't in control of myself.

Upon looking in the Reader, I easily found several ads for "girls." Without thinking, I called one and reached Howard. After a quick phone interview, Howard asked me to come meet him.

I drove about four blocks from my house to a less desirable neighborhood, which in Chicago could mean crossing the street and pulled up to an old two-story brownstone. It was well kept, not dilapidated and although it wasn't inviting, it didn't give off any whorehouse kind of vibe.

After sitting in front of the house for a brief *what-the-fuck-am-I-doing* moment, I got out of the car and walked to the front door. After one more pause and a deep breath, I rang the bell.

A pretty girl, about twenty-two answered the door. "Oh hi, you must be Jess! Howard, Jess is here." she hollered before I could respond. She let me in and directed me to the dining room to meet Howard.

Howard was a small skinny black man that clearly had cirrhosis of the liver as his eyes and fingertips were yellow.

"Hello, you must be Howard," I extended my hand out to shake his, but he didn't take it.

"Hmm, you're pretty thin. Hmm." Howard was circling me, checking out my dimensions. "Why is your hair so short?"

"Um well, I just cut it…."

"Ok, Ok, I am going to have to get a look at you, ya know."

"Wait, what do you mean, you are looking at me now."

"You have any scars or burns or anything?" He asks shortly.

"No." I reply, still standing there like a deer in the headlights.

"Not really any boobs either I see. Hmm." He keeps looking at me. "Ok, I believe you, no scars, usually the girls have to take their clothes off for me so I can make sure, I don't want any cutters or heroin addicts here, you seem ok. Why you want to do this job?"

"Um, I don't know, it just seemed kind of easy I guess."

"Hmm, hey girls, take Jess in the prep room and show her around. Tell her some stories so she knows what she is getting into. Hey, when can you start? Can you start tonight? I think I have someone who would like to meet you."

"Umm, I guess I could start tonight, how does it work, how late do I work, what is the pay and all that stuff?"

"The girls will fill you in, let me know if you want the gig, I think I can use you."

Three girls from the TV room scurried over to show me around. They took me to the bedroom where they all got ready for calls. The closet held countless dresses, jewelry and shoes in various sizes and a two-mirror vanity with makeup and hair supplies spread all over it.

"We all share this stuff so don't worry about bringing your own." Came a voice from a small Asian girl, she pointed to an old twin bed against the wall that held our street clothes. "You can nap here if you want, like if you're here really late or whatever."

"How long are you guys usually here?" I asked.

"We all work different shifts, sometimes I am here til two in the morning." This from the girl who answered the door.

"Oh, I am not a late person, not sure how that is going to go."

"You don't have to, Howard lets you make your own schedule, but he doesn't give you time off for your period, you have to work through it."

"What? How is that even possible?"

"Get a *Today* sponge, it soaks up the blood so you can still fuck, no biggie. Hey, you have to buy your own condoms too, always fucking use a condom, even if you're giving head."

"Ok, so how does a call actually work? ...exactly?"

"So, the first thing you do is call in when you arrive, if anything feels weird, you tell Howard that you are hungry, that's our code for somethings not right, then you either leave the call or stay there. If all is well when you show up, then you basically do what the guy wants; usually just a fuck or head, but sometimes you will find some sicko's; like I had to fuck a guy in the ass with a strap-on once. Sometimes we get sent together, you know two girls and one guy fantasy, they don't even know what to do with two girls most of the time. Sometimes they just want to jack off while they watch us make out or whatever. Anyway, you call in to Howard again before you leave, sometimes Howard will have somewhere else for you to go and sometimes you just come back here." All this came from the girl who answered the door, she was by far the chattiest.

"Keep in mind that if you leave a call, even if it's because you are uncomfortable, Howard wants his money, so if you leave, it comes out of your money for the night one way or another." This was the Asian girl again, she seemed to be the "most senior" girl. "Howard will call the client who gave you trouble and decide if he will put them on the NO SERVICE list, but that's about it."

"Have you guys had anything bad happen to you?" I ask, afraid of the answer.

The three girls agreed that all in all it's a pretty basic gig, nothing bad had happened to any of them. Sometimes the guy was really fat, or the house was dirty, but no one had treated them badly. They spoke more of the wealthy clients with penthouse apartments or the high-end dinners they'd gone to, with foreign businessmen. It seemed each of them had a subtle longing for their journey to unfold into a "Pretty Woman" scenario.

At this point in my life, I did not remember that my mother had been a prostitute. In fact, I had no idea, but it had been imprinted on me, lying deep in my subconscious, waiting to be expressed or healed. I chose the form of self-punishment and re-created my childhood trauma.

In the healing world we call this a Legacy or Generational Trauma. If I don't heal it, I will pass it to my children and so on. This could look like any kind of trauma or life "choice" such as socioeconomic challenges, abusive relationships, choosing partners who don't have time for us just like our parents, the list is endless. My Legacy Trauma manifested as prostitution.

I took the job with Howard as an escort, and he renamed me Andy for business purposes; none of us called each other by our real names. I would show up four nights a week around five o'clock and work till about eleven, usually taking three or four calls a night. It was pretty much what you might expect, six girls sitting around watching TV, ordering food, and waiting for a call while Howard sat in the dining room behind a large elaborate wooden desk covered in piles of paperwork, answering phones, and pitching girls by measurements and hair color.

It was pretty low-key as far as escort services go and I am lucky as fuck to be alive and healthy. I only ever had one call that was really fucked up, it was a new client and Howard told me to pay attention.

When I arrived at the basement apartment door a man in a wheelchair answered. His two young daughters, about four and seven years old were playing just behind him in the tiny living room. Right away I was uncomfortable. I wasn't ok with kids being there and why I didn't turn around and leave right then is beyond me. When I called Howard, there was no answer, so I faked a conversation hoping the man overheard me and knew I had someone watching out for me. I decided the best choice would be to leave but the man blocked my way to the door with his wheelchair.

"Where are you going?" He said beaming with arrogance. He knew I wasn't going to make a scene with his kids right there.

"Howard needs me somewhere else actually, he is going to send someone else."

"I don't think so, I like you, but I have been fooled before, so I am going to need you to prove you're a girl."

"I am sorry, what do you mean?"

"I mean you need to get in that bathroom and take your clothes off and show me you ain't no man."

"I can assure you I am not a man!"

"Prove it!" He was commanding me now.

I walked into the bathroom feeling I had no other options and took off my clothes. "Ok." I called out through the bathroom door.

"Ok what?" He called from the other side of the door.

"Ok, I am done, you can come in if you want."

He opened the door a crack, "Hand me your clothes."

"No, I am going to hold on to my clothes."

He opened the door wider so I could see his children and they could see me standing there naked, "I said, hand me your clothes."

I complied, it was clear he was fucking sick and resisting his commands were going to be worse for all of us. He took my clothes and kept me locked in the bathroom for over an hour, ruminating over what was going to happen next. I remembered when the cabby dropped me off here, he looked into his rearview mirror finding my eyes and said, "Be careful." *How did he know?*

"Hey out there! Howard hasn't heard from me in quite a while, he is going to send someone if I don't call in." I tried not to sound too desperate. Right on cue, the phone rang.

"Girls, turn down that TV while I get the phone here." I could hear him rolling through the house, making his way past the TV. He had been sitting just outside the bathroom door the whole time. "Hello……. Howard, yes hello….no no everything is fine, she is lovely, um, I want to keep her a little longer if that is ok…...Oh uh you can't speak to her now, she is in the bathroom…….Ok, I will get her." Howard had insisted on speaking with me to make sure I was safe, I made him a lot of money, he had an interest in protecting me.

The man opened the door and threw my clothes at me,

"Hurry up and get dressed, you are wasting my time." He was gruff.

I quickly got dressed and rushed to the phone, "Howard, hi-listen I am so hungry, can you pick me up some food please, ASAP!" That was code for I really needed help, send someone to make sure I am ok, call me a cab, anything.

"I already called a cab Andy, are you ok?" Howard was serious, he sounded genuinely worried.

"Yeah, um, ok how do I..." Howard interrupted, "Listen, put him back on the phone, I am going to tell him I need you and that I will send someone else. I am going to tell him you have a cab waiting, that should be enough to get you out of there, you got it?"

"Yep, sounds good Howard," I say in a peppy voice and hand the phone back to the man. As soon as he took the phone I walked straight out the door, I didn't even have my shoes on yet.

When I got back to the house, the other girls rushed me with hugs. Howard had told them I was in trouble. I was overwhelmed and hadn't even really processed the event myself but was grateful for the show of care.

"Hey, Andy, come on in here." Howard poked his head out from around the corner and beckoned me to the dining room to talk.

"Hi Howard, thanks for getting me out of that, he was..." Howard interrupted again, "That was my fault, I had a bad feeling and I sent you anyway, I am sorry about that."

"Oh, thanks for saying that. He was really weird, and his kids were there and...."

"Look Andy, I don't want to hear about it, you are out and safe, done. Now you can have the night off if you want or you can work, I don't care, but I wanted to give you the option. He was your first call of the night, so you are going to owe me if you don't work tonight but I know you're good for it."

"What, I am going to owe you? You just said this was your fault and you shouldn't have sent me!"

"Those are the rules Andy, and you know it, I can't get soft, this is just part of the business." He had his eyes to the floor.

"Yeah, Ok Howard, I will owe you then, I am going home." I couldn't believe what I was hearing.

The charge for an hour of service with me was $200, we split it 60/40, that meant I walked with $120 a pop. I was nineteen and to me the money was great, but what the fuck was I doing? I was totally out of my body.

One day, one of my regulars prepared me a snack and brought me a Pepsi. He knew I liked a particular show on TV, so he put it on, and we started talking. It wasn't until there were only five minutes left in the hour that he motioned toward the bed. From that point forward I started to have a lot of regulars that behaved similarly. Many of them just wanted someone to talk to and some even offered to take me on trips. I started being more present, listening, touching an arm in recognition or compassion.

In truth, this was the first time I consciously became of service, the first time my healing gifts emerged. Certainly, I used some of the listening skills I learned at Echo Ranch in group counseling, but it was more than that. Men began to cry with me and tell me their darkest fears and secrets. I held a safe space for them to let go whatever they needed; it was a nice change from all the sex.

Soon, I rarely had to go on a blind call, my regulars kept me working most nights, which meant less sex and more presence, but still it wasn't good for me.

I lived this strange work life four nights a week and went on with my normal lesbian life the rest of the time, even dating. Not everyone knew what I was doing, but I felt it important to be honest with those I slept with. I think most people just kind of skipped over it, almost like they didn't understand what I was saying, but it worked out ok, I guess.

I think I disassociated with the work most of the time. I wasn't a girl that drank or did drugs to cope (except of course for that month-long stint of coke) I sort of just turned part of myself off in order to do the work and went on living an otherwise normal life.

The biggest consideration for me was disease, I always had with me no less than twenty condoms. Surprisingly, the *Johns* never put up a fight to wear them, I imagine they were just as concerned.

I left Howard in the spring after five months, but five months was plenty of time to recognize I had done some real damage to my soul. I needed to leave and reset, I had to go home to the mountains to get my head on straight. The city was its own kind of drug, drowning out my soul with noise and distraction, I could feel I wasn't going to be able to heal while I was still there.

Sixty Dollar Station Wagon

My Uncle Har, true to form, offered me respite. Har was the savior for all us kids; whenever my cousins got in trouble, they would call him, and he would help them out of whatever jam they were in. For the first time in my life, I did the same.

Har sent my cousins to Chicago to pick me up in an old jacked up Lincoln Continental, I grabbed the few items I had, threw them in the trunk and drove out of the city without looking back, bound for Iowa.

Once we got to my Aunt Linda's house, I helped Har work on an old motorhome we were driving back to Colorado. My job was to paint Kilz, a paint that blocks and covers stains, mildew, and mold along the inside ceiling where there was mold damage. The fumes were brutal in such a tight space, but the heat might have been worse. While I was busy painting, Har was working on the motor, after about a week, we hit the road back to Colorado.

Har took the long way home with a detour to Billings Montana to look at an old dump truck he wanted to buy; it was twelve hours out of the way for a ten-minute stop. Despite the detour, he refused to stop anywhere to spend the night, so we drove through the night, taking turns passing out on the bed in the back of the motorhome. The second night, around two in the morning, he woke me up, "Jess, hey Jess, wake up!"

"What? Ok, I'm up, what time is it?" I sat up but was groggy as fuck.

"I don't know, but I need you to take the wheel, come on, get up here!" Har was pushy.

I got up and moved to the passenger seat, we were on a two-lane mountain pass and low fog stunted our visibility.

"Doesn't look like there is going to be a turn out for a bit." I say, wondering how we are going to switch drivers.

"We don't need a turn out, here take the wheel, I'll scoot behind you, and you can slide into the driver's seat."

"Are you fucking serious? Har, look at this road, it is nothing but tight turns down a steep hill! Also...hello, we are in a huge motorhome that I barely feel comfortable driving, there is no way I am doing this!"

"Yes, you are, or we are going to crash, let's go, here, take the wheel," he let go of the wheel and looked over at me.

"What the fuck Har, we are going to crash!" I jumped out of the passenger seat and went for the wheel, steering while standing just to the side, I was scared shitless.

"No no, you can do this no problem." He was playing a game of chicken with me except he was serious.

"Ok, now I am going to take my foot off the gas and slide right behind you, you can slide right in, no big deal, you got it?" He was a little giddy, which freaked me out.

"No Har, I don't get it, this is FUCKING NUTS!" Then he slid out of the seat, and I had no option but to slide in and start driving.

"See, no problem, I told you you could do it! I am going to go lay down, the brakes are a little soft so give yourself some room to slow down or stop ok, see you in a couple hours." With that he went to the back and laid down.

When we got back to Colorado, Har gave me a place to live on his land in Old Snowmass in a 1970's 5th wheel with no electricity or running water overlooking the Snowmass Monastery. Living so far up in the mountains he thought I should have a vehicle, so he took me to a police auction and bought me a 1982 Ford station wagon with no reverse for only $60.

At first, sitting in solitude on top of a mountain felt lonely, especially after the noise of the city, but eventually I unwound and found great joy in the simplicity that surrounded me.

I had a 360-degree view of mountain range upon mountain range nestled against the sky and could enjoy both sunrise and sunset. My favorite part of the day was stepping outside every morning to rays of sun reaching their light into darkness, waking up the mountains and warming the earth. Sometimes it felt like I waited hours for the sun to break free from the horizon before I grabbed a gallon jug of water to brush my teeth, standing naked in the center of creation. This was just the medicine I needed to come home to myself.

I soon got a job at *The Ritz Carlton* in Aspen, now the *St. Regis*, as a hotel phone operator and worked the night shift. The $60 car my uncle was kind enough to buy me didn't have keys or reverse, but it ran great. Getting keys made was easy enough but we weren't about to change out the transmission to fix the reverse. I just had to park on a hill so I knew I could get out of my parking spot and luckily in Aspen, there are a lot of hills. Sometimes, when I couldn't park on a hill, I would park in the employee lot and have to recruit people off the street to help me push the car out of its place. I got pretty good at being friendly and everyone seemed to enjoy helping me out, especially the drunks late at night. They thought it was hilarious that this skinny little girl had to push her monster station wagon out of a spot.

That car was a beast, an elk jumped out in front of me one night when I was going about 55mph and while it killed the poor animal the only damage to the car was the grill. The vehicle and the living situation were perfect for that time in my life, nothing cost any money or was high maintenance. I could shower at work, solving the biggest challenge of no running water, so I was pretty much set...at least until the snow started to fall.

It became too cold to stay in the 5th wheel past November, so I moved into the loft of my uncle's cabin. The living situation wasn't as ideal, sure, I had water and electricity, but I didn't have any privacy living in an exposed loft with a married couple that fought all the time while a couple of young kids ran around screaming.

To add insult to injury, the station wagon was a fucking sled on the snow, so my uncle had me park it at the bottom of the driveway, two miles below the main house and then drive an old Jeep Wagoneer up to the house. The catch was: **one**, the jeep didn't have a driver side window so when it was snowing, you were getting snowed on and **two**, there was only one battery between both cars, so I had to take the battery out of whatever car I was driving and put it in the car I was about to drive. I got pretty good at this given I did it at least five days a week.

Why I didn't go buy another battery is beyond me...

Eventually, this became very tiresome, and I needed a change. I was lonely without my gay community and isolated on top of a mountain. After about six months, I headed back to Chicago, leaving the station wagon with my uncle, there was no way I was going to park in the city without reverse.

Chapter Eleven

Chicago Part 2 - Charlie

Heading back to the city was simply an act of leaving my uncle's house. I knew I loved the food and the community, but I had no real intention for anything specific in Chicago, just change.

As before, the rush of the city was exhilarating, I went back to all my favorite spots, dancing, eating amazing food and meeting ladies but I was very aimless. These were my early twenties, and I was doing exactly what I was supposed to; but as before, when it came to work in the city, I was paralyzed.

After only a month, I had burned through the money I came with and found myself homeless, begging on the streets. My friends would let me crash at their places, but I couldn't take responsibility for picking myself up. Unfortunately, I once again joined an escort service. A different one this time, a little "higher end" if you will.

My pimp was Ron Jon Steve Brian. I don't know if any of those were his real name but that's what we called him, *almost in jest*. He was in his mid-twenties, blond hair, blue eyes and fit, I could tell though, he was probably picked on in high school.

This time there was no house, Ron Jon Steve Brian just paged us when and where we were needed. Sometimes he would meet us at the call and personally introduce us to people. His clientele was a little more upscale than Howard's; police chiefs, musicians, CEO's, etc. but it was the same gig.

Remarkably for me, a similar pattern played out as before, in that these men wanted my companionship more than my body, even new clients, after engaging in conversation with me, would tell me they couldn't sleep with me.

"Wow, you're so cool, I can't believe you do this. I am not sure I can sleep with you now." Was a common comment.

"Thank you I think... you've already paid me either way." I never knew how to respond. It was a compliment to my personality but a degradation of my character.

Some men were looking for a woman who was willing to be an object, I was simply too human for them. I could only be myself, that is all I have ever been able to do. If they had good music playing for example, I would comment and then a genuine conversation would develop. I couldn't act or pretend to fill some role for these men. Apparently, I was often too normal and even too likable to pound on. I didn't fit the stereotype, yet they called me back, again and again.

Occasionally, I would meet other girls in the service when we were put on calls together. I often got put on calls with a girl I will call Olivia. She was beautiful, long blond hair, blue eyes, and a wide, white smile. Olivia was all about having fun, she was much more interested in the job than I was, and it showed. We tended to have the same couple of repeat client's week after week and eventually became friends.

During one call, Olivia told me that she and her boyfriend just bought themselves a Golden Retriever puppy they named Charlie. As a dog lover, I was excited and asked her questions about how he was doing every time we worked together and even went to her house a few times to visit him.

Every time I arrived at her house; Charlie was in his kennel. Olivia had shared with me that they were doing kennel training, but it was clear they didn't know what that actually meant. Olivia thought I would just pet him through the open squares in his kennel but of course that was ridiculous.

"What's he doing in there, let him out!" I would say as Charlie perked up his ears and wagged his tail.

Rolling her eyes, Olivia would let him out and then jump back knowing what was about to happen. Immediately Charlie would get excited and pee all over the place...A LOT!

"That's why we keep him in there!" Olivia was exasperated.

Admittedly, Charlie's bladder was a little overwhelming, even so, I offered to take him on walks and when we came back, I always refilled the empty water dish before putting him back in his kennel.

A few months have passed when Olivia and I find ourselves at a new client's house and as part of the pre-game "chit-chat" she tells us, me, and the *John*, how her puppy Charlie got into some acid over Thanksgiving and how funny it was. How he fell down the stairs because he was having such a hard time walking and orienting. The truth, I later found out, was that Jimmy, her boyfriend had "nudged" him down the outside metal stairs of their house, because he too, was tripping his balls off and didn't want to have to go outside and walk him.

"That's so fucked-up!" I say staring at her with my eyes and mouth wide open.

I think she thinks I am kidding because she laughs, but the *John* says nothing and motions to us it's time to get on with it.

I see Olivia again the following week at the same client's house, he always calls for both of us which is kind of refreshing because we know our roles and it makes it easier to push through a couple of hours with this guy.

As we are leaving the call, Olivia asks me if I want to watch Charlie while she and her boyfriend go out of town. I was lucky to live in an apartment that allowed dogs, so I happily said **"yes!"**

Charlie still wasn't housebroken at six months and demonstrated terrible anxiety for most things but especially loud noises, which led him to involuntarily pee all over everything all the time. If I raised my voice in frustration there would be pee, if I moved quickly toward him, more pee. There was no way to train him because he was afraid of everything, so I did my best to get him out every two hours in an effort to empty his bladder outside as often as possible.

The challenge with this tactic in the beginning was that he was too scared to pee outside. The stimulus that was the city was just too much for him and he simply couldn't relax outside. Inevitably once we came back inside and got into the elevator, Charlie peed. I quickly grew accustomed to bringing paper towels and plastic bags with us every time we went out.

Even with Charlie's pee problem, I loved him deeply; he

needed a good home where someone would see him and be kind to him, not some bimbo who let him eat acid when he was four months old and then laughed about it.

It was clear these people had no idea how to raise a dog. I didn't really know how to tell Olivia that I didn't think she should keep him, all I knew was I couldn't give him back and as the week drew to a close, I became really nervous about how this was all going to go down.

The end of the week came and went but Olivia didn't call... so I didn't call. About three weeks later Olivia and I ended up at one of our regulars together. I was surprised to see her, someone else had been filling in for her for quite some time, but she didn't mention anything about Charlie.

As we were leaving, I gently brought up the subject.

"You were gone a lot longer than I thought," I say as I put on my winter jacket over my slinky dress.

"Yeah, we had a great time and just decided to stay at the beach a little longer." Still no mention of Charlie.

"Ok, well, you know I love Charlie and I would really love it if he could stay with me longer." I say this sort of casually, like borrowing a sweater.

"Oh yeah, I knew you'd want to keep him, I am so glad, he was sooooo much work. He will be happier with you. Ok see you next time." Then she hopped in a cab and was gone.

I stood silent in the cold while a light snow fell all around me. I was in disbelief for a moment before a wave of love came over me. Charlie was mine? Charlie was mine...**Charlie was MINE!!!!!**

Once I absorbed what had happened, I rushed to the

corner to catch a cab, I couldn't wait to get home and hold that dog!

When I got home, I surrendered to Charlie, holding him while I cried and he too surrendered, relaxing into my arms and for the first time, he didn't pee. In that moment, we understood that we were there for each other, forever. Charlie gave me a love I had never experienced before, his sweet soul shone a light so bright that it pierced right through my bullshit and straight into my heart, helping me remember my own light.

It was because of Charlie; I left the sex industry. Somehow, this dog made me want to be and do better for him than I was doing for myself. But I had to work, and my next best effort turned out to be, of all things, selling fur on Michigan Avenue.

Going back to selling fur didn't seem any better than prostitution and to top it off I was gone from Charlie for eight hours at a time. It wasn't going to work, and I didn't last a month. The problem was I was still paralyzed when it came to finding a job in Chicago, there was only one option... Colorado.

Chapter Eleven

Remembering

After a long fifteen-hour drive in an old Subaru I had bought before leaving my Uncle Har's, I found myself sitting back in the driveway of my grandfather's house.

By this time in the evolution of the fur business, my grandfather spent most of his summers at his horse ranch in Texas. This meant his home in East Vail was vacant for me to live in for the summer.

As I sat in the driveway, I could see there was still snow on the north facing hill that led down to the creek. I rejoiced with tears as I turned off the ignition and sat for a moment just letting go. Everything I loved about the city had no hold on me now, for some reason the only thing that mattered to me was taking care of Charlie.

A few moments passed as the weight of Chicago lifted from my body and then, as if I couldn't wait one more second, I quickly got out of the car and invited Charlie to come with me to check out his new digs.

Even now, after all these years the approach to the house was uncomfortable, it was like walking into the darkness before finding the light that waited on the other side of the door. We walked the long dark wooden hallway cautiously, pausing at the front door before trying the handle, it was unlocked as usual.

As I opened the door, light poured over us like a baptism, signaling our freedom to rest. It was as though I never left, the trees that stood outside like guardians, greeted me with knowing groundedness. I felt it as real as an elder's hand on my shoulder, signaling it was all going to be ok.

I had the opportunity to go by this home recently and happened upon the caretaker who kindly let me in to look around. It was more magnificent than I remembered, and it was as though every cell in my body lit up with a familiar resonance. It felt like the creek itself experienced a similar phenomenon, rejoicing in recognition of my presence as it reached up and plugged itself into my second chakra. All at once I understood my connection to the land and all it held me through. The wisdom that it imparted on me while I slept and the secrets it whispered to my soul every time I sought refuge here.

I cried the entire hour and a half drive back to my home in Carbondale, not tears of sorrow but tears of connection, understanding and appreciation.

Charlie was clearly at ease as he followed my lead moving through the house, taking time to sniff every corner. When I walked him out the sliding glass door to show him the creek, he was visibly scared. *That's good, I thought; I didn't have to worry about him getting swept away in the fast-moving spring current.* We walked around the perimeter of the house, letting him get to know his surroundings before returning inside and sitting for a moment.

We were home, we were safe, we were together.

Not long after our move out west, Charlie's pee challenge seemed to vanish. There were times when he would get really excited and have a little bit of an accident, but nothing like before. I know it was the peace that he found in Colorado and the love that he received from me. Soon, he would not need a leash and would begin to understand me and what I asked of him in every way.

Forgiveness

After decompressing in quiet and stillness for a few days, I reached out to my mom. We hadn't seen each other in years, we had talked a few times but neither of us had treated the other with very much kindness in a long time. That said, she had gotten the ok for me to move to the East Vail house and I was grateful.

Because she had recently separated from David, I was able to visit her on her eighty acre ranch in Eagle where David had once banned me for being gay. We sat on the front porch swing watching the horses in the pasture, it was a somewhat neutral space to try and reconnect. After sitting in silence for a long time I apologized to her for how I treated her and she too, apologized to me. We sat there for a while longer not saying much before I told her what I was walking away from in Chicago.

"Mom, listen, I know you think being a lesbian is a phase, but it's really where I feel most comfortable. Is it really that big a deal to you?"

"No honey, I don't care, but David does, he just wasn't raised with that kind of freedom in his thinking." She was genuine, but still deflecting any responsibility.

"But you didn't stick up for me." I say a little too sharply.

"I know, I am sorry, he was really scared you would influence Chad somehow."

"Seriously? That's fucking stupid! Listen, I want to tell you something, but it's really hard."

"What is it, Jessica?"

"Look, um.... when I was in Chicago, I had kind of a hard time finding a job."

"That's unlike you, you've been working since you were fourteen."

"I know, I know! It was weird, but anyway, I couldn't do it or whatever and I.... I worked for an escort service." If she didn't take me being a lesbian very well, this was surely going to get me kicked out of the family for good.

My mom broke down crying, "I am so sorry honey, I am so sorry."

"Mom, what are you sorry for, I am sorry." I started crying too, Charlie put his head on my lap to comfort me.

She moved in closer for a hug, but I wasn't ready and pulled back, "Jessica this is all my fault, you don't understand."

"How is this your fault? Mom, I am such an idiot, I am so sorry."

But she kept crying and apologizing to me, "This is all my fault."

I could feel her response wasn't really about me, I mean it was, but there was clearly something deeper, I could feel that.

"It was me, I did it too, when you were a baby, I am so sorry honey."

I was floored and moreover, as my mom was telling me her story, the truth of it became alive in my memory. I see it in her as well, this imprint or story is written all over her, I can't explain how I see it but it is in front of me like a movie trailer...and then I see me, very young in the backseat of a car and then I go right back to the memory I have always held, the one I know too well and it all came flooding back.

There wasn't much else to say after that, so I loaded Charlie in the car and drove back to East Vail.

I think I sat in that house for three full days, trying to process what she said, what I remembered and the choices I made in Chicago. I didn't hike, I didn't talk to anyone, I sat in one chair, looking out the windows at the trees and the creek, I just processed. It wasn't like I was processing in the brain, trying to make sense of it; it was more of a whole mind, body spirit kind of thing...a letting go, and perhaps a forgiveness. I didn't really understand it, it was new to me but yet, it was familiar.

Finally, after three days, I sobbed, I mean I sobbed the kind of face down on the kitchen floor kind of sob, where primal screams of suffering get released and pain moves through you in such a way that you almost welcome it. The kind of sob where your insides actually ache in a way you never thought possible, the kind of sob that tells you, you are alive.

Those moments on the kitchen floor allowed me to let go of the guilt and blame for what I had done to myself. My mom's confession brought me an understanding of my choices and I forgave myself. I held so much gratitude that I had been safe, remained healthy and got out of it alive.

The remembrance of my mom's suffering also gave me a new perspective on how she had been made to move through this world. She never had support, education or even family on her side; instead, she was everyone's scapegoat, the person to blame and dismiss because she was "crazy." Even though she worked her ass off and built her life from nothing, even though she lent money to everyone and never got paid back, even though she wanted nothing more than a family, she was always the one to be made wrong. For the first time maybe ever, I saw her and felt genuine compassion. It was a turning point for us and we started to rebuild our relationship.

As the light started coming back to my heart, I was drawn back outside. I didn't want to engage much with the world, so Charlie and I sat by the creek for hours, letting the water carry away what was left of our pain. We sat and sat until finally one day, maybe a week later, it was time to move.

I began hiking again, slowly, I was still a smoker and when you combine altitude and smoker lungs, it's pretty slow going. I decided after a particularly difficult hike that smoking was dumb, I was tired of smelling like ass, so I stopped cold turkey. That was it, I wasn't hanging around smokers like I did in Chicago, there was no pressure to belong or conform and my true self just wasn't a smoker. It was easy actually; I was glad to be done with it.

My health improved quickly, and I found I had a ton of time on my hands I didn't really know what to do with, so I hiked more, exploring high alpine trails, waterfalls, and Aspen groves. I had some money saved up from when I was in Chicago and was able to take care of myself for most of the summer. I eventually got a part-time job at the Marriott as an in-room dining server. It was perfect for Charlie, I worked from 5:30 a.m. until 11 a.m. so he didn't have to be home alone much, and I was able to make a little extra cash for whatever was to come next.

As fall approached, it was time to figure out a housing situation, my grandfather would be back for the winter season (mountain town economies are defined by "season") and he decidedly didn't like pets, plus, I wanted my own space.

The Minturn Years

My boyfriend Mike, from pre-Chicago days and I naturally reconnected when I moved back to the area, and he let me know his neighbors were moving out. I asked him to put in a good word for me with the landlord in hopes I could get the cute little mining shack next door to his double wide in the town of Minturn.

Minturn had so far escaped the money, development, and influence of the Vail Valley. I knew it well from my days in middle school and from my time with Mike from the past, I felt very at home here. Minturn was an old school, blue collar, migrant town, two miles long and four blocks wide, built along a narrow river valley. The train ran alongside the river with its rhythmic roar and high-pitched squeal of metal on metal twice a day. I loved the sound of the train, especially in the winter when the coyotes would howl and yip as it went by; it was as eerie as it was awesome.

Gratefully, I was able to rent the old mining shack next to Mike's house and begin rebuilding my life in earnest. It was small, maybe 1,000 square feet, but it was mine. The house was constructed of old railroad ties which provided no insulation and what's worse were the windows as thin as those on an old school bus. The cast iron wood burning stove that lived in the corner was not only the main heat source but the object of my affection; perhaps because it brought back memories of my youth. I found a peaceful rhythm in preparing the wood and stoking the fire. If I wanted to be warm, I had to stoke that stove first thing in the morning and last thing at night. Even so, it was not unusual to wake up with a quarter inch of ice on the inside of the windows.

I was grateful my mother brought over an extra cord of old barnwood from a dilapidated shed off her property that first winter, had she not, I would have been short wood that year.

That same winter, Colorado had a record snow year, 422 inches. The snow was so tall it met the roof line of the house in one corner; it was very convenient, actually, because I had to get up on the roof and shovel weekly to keep it from caving in. I remember the icicles that formed out the kitchen window that year went from the roof to the ground and were as thick as my leg. For me and for those around me, it was **heaven!**

The house had a small, fenced yard that joined with Mike's house, perfect for Charlie. Mike was a dog guy too and he and I had gotten him a black lab mix named Sadie, back when we were dating. Sadie was now only six or so but was dying of cancer that presented itself on her tongue. In an effort to rid her body of cancer, the vet recommended we cut as much of her tongue off as possible while still giving her the ability to eat and hopefully drink. Consequently, she ended up with a short skinny tongue that allowed her to eat but made it difficult to lap up water. We got her a special water bottle and helped her drink for the rest of her life.

For some reason, Sadie preferred staying at my house those last months of her life. Mike was a little sad, but it felt right, even to him. I think maybe having Charlie's healing soul near her was part of it. When she showed us her pain was becoming too much, we put her down and buried her on my mom's ranch, something I am still grateful for today. My mom can be difficult, but she can also have a beautiful heart.

Despite this difficult time with Sadie, Charlie and I continued to thrive in Minturn. I had left the Marriott and now spent four nights a week selling cashmere and two days in my mom's fur store in Vail. It was a time in my life where I could easily live off of $1200 a month yet made plenty more and spent every penny going to concerts at Red Rocks.

The schedule made it easy for me to spend my days outside with Charlie, snowshoeing in the winter and hiking in the summer. Our crew would play volleyball every Wednesday and on Mondays I would take an all-day hike with a friend and his Malamute, Nikki deep into the mountains. These were times of bliss and ease for me.

Charlie and I got into the habit of hiking every morning by eight. There was a great trailhead just two-minutes from our house where we could head up for an hour or hike all day long. The trail traversed a landscape first of rolling meadows and dilapidated shepherd cabins, then to thick Aspens and finally a dense evergreen forest alongside Grouse Creek, which provided a great water source for Charlie. After four hours, the trail opened up to a wide meadow of wildflowers surrounding a high alpine lake. It was stunning!

All this hiking was really bringing me back into my body and the time spent amongst the trees and creeks continued to cleanse and nurture my soul. I was so grateful to be alive; to have the absolute privilege to hike these mountains and heal these deep broken parts of myself in a way that also brought me joy.

The only challenge with being back in Colorado was the "gay scene" or lack thereof. Especially back then, there were a handful of gay men, but it was tough to spot the lesbians. "Gaydar" isn't as effective in the mountains when lots of girls are "*sporty*."

Can you believe the generalizations I am using, don't get your panties in a bunch, it's ok!

It didn't really matter too much as I was pretty fulfilled hiking with my dog and hanging out with friends. Mike and I naturally fell back together, and it felt pretty good. There wasn't a word then other than bisexual to "explain" my sexuality and I caught a lot of heat about it from my lesbian friends...which I didn't understand.

Why would a group of people who are routinely discriminated against discriminate against me for what I enjoyed in my heart and in my bed? Lesbians at that time could be a little uptight and judgmental. Today we understand that sexuality can be fluid, I really like that word for it.

I turned twenty-four the second year I was in the mining shack and although this had been by far the best time of my life, I saw limitations in its longevity. I started to ask questions of the future: *How long can I live like this, what more do I want out of life, what does my career look like?*

And once again, I was called back to Chicago.

Chapter Twelve

Chicago Part 3 - Third Time's A Charm

I was a little nervous about bringing Charlie back to the city, he was so happy in Colorado, but I trusted what was right for me would be right for him. Indeed, the noise no longer bothered him, and we found walking along Foster Beach every morning for an hour was a good substitute for hiking in the mountains. This time we made the city work for us.

Upon my return to Chicago, I met a mesmerizing woman named Ripley, with long dark hair and big brown eyes. She had a bit of an edge to her, but like others I had been attracted to, she was a musician.

Fuck, those musicians get me every time!

She seemed mysterious and funky, pushing harder against society's norms than I did. I hadn't met anyone else like that, so I thought we were a match made in heaven. I was drawn to her, but there were also strange little things that made me question. For example, her anger would pop up out of nowhere and often seemed excessive for the circumstance. While in the beginning, her anger wasn't directed at me, that eventually changed, and she wound up breaking me down into a shadow of myself.

It's interesting to look back and explore how I became an emotionally abused woman. I don't even think Ripley was doing it intentionally, but somehow my inner strength gave way to an insecure fool.

The first time Ripley lost her temper, we were going to see a matinee. The advertised ticket price in the *Reader* was less than what the guy behind the window was charging us and she lost her shit. Ripley was full on yelling at this guy and all I could do was stand there trying to make sense of what I was seeing. I would have paid the extra two dollars to avoid a scene and continue with my day, but Ripley took it personally somehow and ripped this guy a new one. It was one of those times when you don't know how to react because what you're seeing either doesn't make sense or you have no context for it; for me, it was both.

I was confused leaving the movie theater, we opted for lunch instead and I was silent as we walked to the restaurant. There was definitely tension in the air as we made our way to our table at Penny's Noodles. *Yay, I thought to myself, Pad See Ew!*

After ordering, my first inclination was to ask why the incident upset her so much and suggest she might be overreacting.

I opened with, "So that was pretty intense."

"Fucking idots!" she seethed, obviously still reeling from the encounter.

"I mean, it was only like two bucks, I don't really

understand, it's not like they were pocketing our money for themselves."

"Are you fucking serious Jess, they shouldn't advertise the price if they aren't going to honor it!"

"Ok, but sometimes, mistakes are made, it wasn't likely the mistake of the two ticket sellers that you went off on."

"Those assholes could have sold us the tickets for less, but they wouldn't, slave to the fucking man!"

"I don't know Rip, that seemed a little intense for the circumstances."

We ate the rest of the meal in awkward silence.

After going to one of Ripley's gigs, I was in, all the way, headfirst. She was so fucking hot on stage, I couldn't tare myself away. I became her roadie, helping her carry equipment in and out of gigs and stood on the sidelines beaming with pride as she sang her heart out. There were more angry outbursts, but I was so drawn to her I looked past it.

Ripley would never hurt an animal, but still, Charlie would show me he was scared of her. He trembled in the corner during angry outbursts, like when she flipped over the dining room table or threw a shoe at my head. I saw him shaking, I saw him, and I knew I needed to get out of this relationship; but I was hooked, like I was underwater, and she was my lifeline.

At the same time however, I was drawn to exploring what was next in my life. I had finally been able to get an above-board job in the city as a caregiver for a man named Patrick who was a paraplegic. It was through caring for this man that I was exposed to alternative healing methods such as Feldenkrais and Healing Touch. His practitioners felt it was beneficial for him to receive some form of treatment every day and taught me basic techniques to apply to Patrick between his weekly appointments. It was this small exposure to alternative healing that lit a fire in my heart and propelled me to explore my calling.

One such exploration brought me to Hampshire College in the Northeast part of the country in Amherst, Massachusetts. Hampshire is a small, student driven, experiential liberal arts school that intrigued me. I still wasn't sure what I wanted to study, but the freedom to be curious and shape my destiny resonated.

I decided to take Charlie on a ten-day road trip out east to visit the school, stopping by a friend's cabin in Lake Chautauqua on the way. I was excited to explore that part of the country, especially in the fall.

It was routine for me to leave Chicago for a couple of days and go camping with Charlie in order to balance my need for nature with my need for the city. Remarkably, there are several beautiful state parks relatively close to Chicago. There weren't mountains, but there were lush forests and small waterfalls that held my attention enough to make it worth my while.

Ripley had never been camping or seen mountains, she didn't understand my need for nature like I didn't understand her need to freak the fuck out and scream at people for no apparent reason. So, I decided to invite her on this road trip with me, perhaps a little nature would calm her temper.

"Hey Rip, would you like to come on this road trip out east with us for ten days?" I asked over a breakfast of sweet potato burritos at Leo's.

"You want to take ten days off of work just to explore some college to see if you want to go?" Ripley was a little condescending; she was afraid if I liked Hampshire College, I would leave Chicago and her.

"Yes, I have never been out there, and I understand the fall colors are magnificent, plus there are all kinds of trees I have never even seen before!"

"Who does that? I can't just leave for ten days!"

"Why?" I say, a little amused she is getting so worked up.

This is when she remembers she is a self-employed bookkeeper and musician...in fact, she can take time off. So Ripley drove east with Charlie and me, off to explore the unknown. I'm pretty sure she was terrified, this was a totally new concept for her, except she was a traveling musician, so it wasn't.

Upon waking up in our first campsite, Ripley spotted a walking stick bug. "Shit, Jess, that stick is moving, what the hell is going on?"

"Oh, yeah, that's just a walking stick bug, pretty cool right?"

"Oh my God, I can't, I mean I really can't, you need to do something with that thing."

"What do you mean it's walking on a branch like six feet away from you."

"Kill it, get it, I don't know, do something."

"Wait a minute, are you afraid of that thing, it moves so slowly, and it isn't interested in you at all."

"It's freaking me out Jess!"

"Then walk away from it Rip."

"Oh my God, is it going to like jump or fly at me or something when I move?"

"No, it's a walking stick, it just moves along slowly on branches, it can't hurt you, like it can't!"

Ripley ran to me, her body tensed up and her arms pulled in over her chest.

"Jesus Rip, are you serious with this, is it just because you haven't seen one of those or is it like all bugs."

"All bugs, alllllllll bugs, I hate bugs!!!"

"That might be a problem sister, we are camping almost every night."

"Fuck no, I can't, this is not going to work."

"Listen Ripley, that's non-negotiable, I love camping, I love nature, I even love most bugs. I never kill spiders; I just move them outside. I love watching bees, ants and all sorts of things, everything has a purpose. You are going to have to figure this out babe." I had sacrificed some of my self-worth to be with this woman, I wasn't going to sacrifice my time in nature.

Ripley threw a temper tantrum like a child, stomping her feet and whining in frustration, but then, she just stopped and figured it out. This didn't mean she was going to rescue a spider and put it outside or be able to deal with bugs in general, but she stopped freaking out and asked for help if there was an insect nearby. This was a vast improvement from her angry outbursts every time an insect was near, and her decision showed me that I was important to her.

The northeast was different from anything I had experienced; the colors on the trees were so vibrant they almost appeared luminescent. Canopies of yellow, orange, and red sheltered our way like a tunnel through quaint country towns and narrow winding roads. The air was cool and crisp, but the vibration of the land was entirely different from the land in Colorado or Illinois, perhaps it felt older somehow.

We hiked up the face of ski hills, on fire with color and crossed sweet mountain streams as fresh as the one's in Colorado. I found a new place of beauty, perhaps it wasn't my resonate match, but I deeply appreciated it just the same.

My visit and interview at Hampshire College was eye opening, more than anything it illustrated the endless ways in which I could educate myself. Hampshire College was created to break the norms of higher education, discouraging standard learning practices while encouraging a model of curiosity, humility, confidence, and problem solving. This idea spoke to me in every way, it was incredible to think I could follow my curiosity and it could lead me to a purposeful career. The college itself was not quite the right fit, partially due to its location, so far from Colorado and partially because it was super expensive, but the experience and ideas I came away with were well worth the 900-mile drive.

After spending two days in Amherst, we headed back to Chicago, choosing a route that took us through the Finger Lakes in eastern New York. The Finger Lakes are a set of eleven lakes, carved from receding glaciers, resembling a large set of fingers on the land, it was in this spot that Ripley finally fell in love with camping.

Nick Drake was playing on the radio while I was making dinner on a single burner camp stove perched atop a picnic table. The fall colors were going off as far as the eye could see and acorns were falling from the trees like rain. This moment softened her and her whole being shifted, she was all in.

Ripley had been watching me make fires the entire trip and decided it was her turn to try. She asked me not to help unless she asked, and I agreed. I watched as she crumpled the newspaper, chopped the wood down to make kindling and then made a tipi out of that kindling on top of the paper. She prepared small pieces of wood to put on top once the fire caught. It was clear she had studied me while I prepared our fires morning and night on our trip, it was satisfying.

After great care to build the right foundation, Ripley struck a match lighting three sides. She was nervous, I could see that, but she was hopeful too.

It was working; the fire caught, and Ripley squealed with delight.

"Ok, ok, when do I put these bigger logs on, what do I do now, oh my God, it's going to fall!" she screamed out.

"You got it girl, don't worry, it's hot, just make sure there is space for air and stack the logs, so they are stable."

The fire took and Ripley was visibly pleased with herself. From that point forward, Ripley came camping with me almost every time I left the city. I was so happy to have exposed her to the outdoors and even happier that she liked it.

A Spiritual Education

After visiting Hampshire College, I no longer felt it necessary to obtain a four-year degree in something like psychology or architecture. My mother had generously offered to pay for my tuition, within reason, but since I still wasn't clear on what a non-formal education might look like, I began to reflect on questions like: *How do I enjoy spending my time? What is meaningful to me? What am I good at?*

I knew I liked to help people through touch, something I learned supporting Patrick and I also seemed to be naturally gifted in holding space and listening to the deepest parts of people's lives, something I learned as a sex worker. I wondered how I might combine the two.

Eventually I landed on massage school, though I could feel it wasn't quite right, it was my best bet forward. After researching several schools in the Chicago area, I decided on *The Wellness and Massage Training Institute* in Woodridge, IL, just outside of Chicago. I didn't know it at the time, but this decision would change the course of the rest of my life.

When I first toured the school, I was almost in a daze, unsure of what I was doing there, I didn't really want to be a massage therapist. As I read about classes they offered, I saw two columns, one for Massage Therapy and another for Chinese Medicine and Asian Bodywork Therapy. Although I couldn't pronounce many of the classes in the Chinese Medicine curriculum, I was drawn to them. I kept running my finger over the words, *"The Tao of Touch,"* *hmmm that feels* *really good in my body...." The Tao of Touch," I wonder what that means...*The resonance of the words felt familiar somehow and when filling out the paperwork for course study, I checked the box for Chinese Medicine and Asian Bodywork Therapy, not massage.

In my first semester, I participated in my studies like I was moving underwater. I didn't understand what was being taught, but I showed up and worked hard just the same, it was very much like learning a new language. It wasn't until sometime in the second semester that I "woke up" and became alive and deeply interested in what I was learning.

School is where my first intentional healing journeys took place. I studied the Fundamentals of Classical Chinese Medicine, Tui Na, Shiatsu, Eastern Nutrition, Qi Gong and best of all, Jin Shin Do®, translated, The Way of The Compassionate Spirit.

Jin Shin Do® Bodymind Acupressure® was developed by Iona Marsaa Teeguarden, M.A., LMFT beginning in 1976. It follows a beautiful thread rooted in both ancient Chinese Medicine and Jin Shin Jyutsu, offering healing most profoundly in the emotional and spiritual body. Learning and experiencing Jin Shin Do® was perhaps the biggest turning point in my life. The practice has a beautiful listening quality that must be learned in order to be of service, it was much like the listening I did in the forest as a child, and it came naturally.

The Wellness and Massage Training Institute offered a well-rounded curriculum that matched its intellectual expectation with the art of Chinese Medicine. I found the more heady classes like anatomy and kinesiology to be a bit harder, but still very engaging, earning mostly B's. It was the hands-on classes where I shined, when practicing points and channels on my peers for example, the body would call me to the right point. It was sometimes harder for me to remember the names of the 361 points, but I would always be able to accurately find the right point for the task.

Authorized Jin Shin Do® Teacher, Renee Ryan, taught me how to ground into the earth, become an empty vessel and create a connection from the core of the earth through my heart, then my crown to the Divine. This served two purposes; grounding taught me how to protect myself from taking on others' energy while becoming an empty vessel meant I was then a clear channel for God's healing love and light. Renee reminded me to hold safe space, honoring each person's journey as sacred.

Holding safe space is probably the thing I am best at, I do it unconsciously, it is simply part of me. I soon learned that my touch too, was impactful for reasons I couldn't explain. The evidence was clear by the number of my peers who would collapse into healing tears under my hands and arise "lighter" and more fully their true selves.

The process looks like this: As I hold space and gently touch the body, the client's healing begins, letting go of what is no longer of service and opening to Divine Self Love. Next, connection to Spirit is felt and understood, if even for a moment. That spark of love and connection, that remembering that we are not separate, is one of the most beautiful experiences to witness and it brings me to my knees every time.

Unconscious Coupling

After about a year together, Ripley and I got engaged. I can't remember who asked who but pretty early on I knew I was making a mistake.

Ripley was actually really good to me, yes, she had a temper, but she also had a kind and thoughtful soul. One of the most meaningful things she taught me was to "see" people. If we were at the grocery store for example, she read the clerk's name tag and called them by name. If we were out to dinner, she took the time to get to know the server and even made a point to learn the names of the local homeless people near where we lived. Ripley had a tremendous heart; the challenge was that I had to compromise some part of myself to be with her and I never felt truly at ease. That was never Ripley's responsibility to hold, but mine and even so, I agreed to marry her.

While Ripley and I were back in Colorado on a scouting trip for the wedding location, my mom offered to host the reception at her ranch and take care of the flowers. I was hesitant, I didn't want to count on her for anything, but after seeing how excited she was and how easily she and Ripley got along, I agreed.

My mom had recently started dating a man named Cody after first hiring him as a ranch hand. He could fix just about anything and as anyone who has ever had a ranch can tell you, that's necessary. They quickly hit it off and he had recently moved up into the main house with my mom. She said jump and he said, "how high," the dynamic was perfect for my mom, and he seemed to always want to please her, so it worked...at least for now.

My mom got to work giving Cody a list of "to do" items to prepare for the reception which included adding a sunroom onto the back of her house in a three-month time frame, he was happy to comply.

I knew I wanted to get married outside so I took Ripley to my favorite hiking spots around Minturn. We found the perfect spot on Grouse Creek, a short distance up the main trail was a smaller trail bending right that led to a creek crossing and opened into a meadow. We agreed this would be the place, not too far a hike for the older folks from Chicago but just far enough that we were surrounded by nature's grandeur.

Before we left, both my mom and Cody assured us the sunroom addition would be done and ready for the reception. Cody already felt like family, and they were quite sweet with each other, it was nice to see my mom happy.

On our way to Denver International Airport, I cried, as I always did when leaving the mountains. I was making the choice to live in Chicago and although there was a lot of good that was coming out of it, saying goodbye to my mountains was like saying goodbye to part of my soul.

About eight miles from the airport a car in front of us lost control. I don't know how, but all of a sudden it was flipping fifteen feet in the air before landing with a thud in a dirt field just off the road. From the road we could see that the passengers head had hit the windshield, leaving a huge spider web of crushed glass. I made Ripley pull over and ran to the car to see if I could help.

Throughout my life I have carried a CPR / First Aid card and help whenever needed, but this was easily the scariest situation I had ever dealt with. When I got the driver's door open, I found a pregnant woman in shock with a huge laceration on her shoulder. I knew that cuts near the shoulder could be very dangerous, and I wasn't sure if I should move her but I was also genuinely afraid the car was going to blow up. I decided it was best to move away from the car and tried to make her comfortable on the ground as we waited for the ambulance. I gave her some gentle acupressure for shock while I held space for light. She begged me to check on her boyfriend, who I knew was dead, but because I wasn't ready to tell this poor woman the truth, I walked over to the car, reached through the open window, and checked for a pulse on his broken neck. I still don't know why I did this, but I guess I needed a minute to figure out what to say.

Unfortunately, while I was gathering my thoughts, some jackass trying to be important rushed over and was like "Holy shit this guy is dead!" There was no concern for her or her fragile physical and emotional state. Not that I would have said something different, but I would have held her hand, stroked her hair and told her gently.

Around this time the ambulance arrived, Ripley pointed to her wrist indicating we were tight on time, so reluctantly I left, there was nothing more I could do anyway. Getting back in the car I realized how late it was, I couldn't believe how long we had been there, almost an hour. We were going to have to hustle to return our rental car and make our plane back to Chicago.

After returning the rental car, we managed to catch the last airport shuttle for thirty minutes. Ripley and I sat panting from the series of events that had just unfolded when I started to notice my hands and my clothes were covered in blood. I hadn't noticed it before, but it was even on my shoes, but there was nothing I could do but just sit in it.

By the time the shuttle arrived at the airport we had only thirty minutes to make it to the gate, it wasn't impossible in pre 9/11 days but it wasn't easy either. We managed to clear security quickly and ran through the airport to our gate, just making the final boarding call. There hadn't been time to stop and wash my hands, something I couldn't help but notice when I went to buckle my seatbelt.

Once the plane was in the air and the seatbelt sign was off, I went to the bathroom to try and clean up. I watched the dried blood from under my nails bleed pink in the sink and lost it. *I mean, someone died in front of me, and I still tried to normalize the event and make a flight? What the hell just happened?* I cried for the fullness of it all, the rush, the soul who passed and the woman in the field. I cried because something about the whole experience felt peaceful and natural in the truest sense. As I stood there in the tiny airplane bathroom under the fluorescent light, I remembered exactly what I saw and felt as the accident unfolded in front of me. This is when I noticed that I knew when the passenger in the car had died. I felt his spirit leave his body, even before his head went through the windshield. I noticed that there was help there for both the woman and the man as spirits surrounded them.

I was in awe of this new understanding and as I sat quietly with it for a moment, the trauma of the event diminished. I became preoccupied with witnessing the spirit leave the man and the understanding of the other souls present. This experience would sit with me for a long time and eventually helped me learn to lean into my gifts as a healer. I recall the story again now as I move towards my work in mediumship.

The wedding went off without a hitch and my mom pulled through with the flowers and the reception. Tons of our friends from Chicago came out, excited for the excuse to explore Colorado and many of them camped on my mom's property. She came through in every way for us that day and also surprised us with a family trip to Mexico as a gift, saying we could work around my school schedule and go when it was convenient for me.

We decided to go to Mexico over my spring break which was just as the mountain was closing in Vail, meaning it would be off season and easier for my mom to get away. Ripley and I flew into Denver and met Chad, Cody, and my mom at the airport where we all caught the same flight to Mexico together.

Once we arrived at our accommodations, the plan was to hit the bar...*well that was everyone else's plan, my plan was to walk on the beach.* After catching up to everyone thirty minutes later, I found my mother was already drunk. I shrugged it off as a long day of travel and not enough food.

My mom had gotten us two rooms for the trip, one for Ripley and I and another that she, Cody, and my brother shared. We were in Playa Del Carmen, a relatively new destination area at the time. It offered us easy access to Mayan ruins, swimming with dolphins, boats to Cozumel, deep sea fishing and my favorite, snorkeling at Xel Ha near Tulum. Xel Ha offers some of the most diverse snorkeling in the world, located between the Caribbean and along the River Maya, Xel Ha provides the opportunity to snorkel from a freshwater river into a biodiverse saltwater bay and it was amazing!

We entered the River Maya at the edge of a dense Mangrove Forest, rich with life. At first the Mangrove Trees freaked me out, the exposed twisted root system looked otherworldly to me. There were fish of every size and color swimming near the roots, reflecting the sunlight in their scales before darting into the root system and feeding on the insects that sought protection under their shade.

The Mangroves are a vital part of the transitional ecosystem here, offering food, habitat, and water purification. We were instructed not to touch them or use them for support as we moved through the water. Although the Mangroves were tough and could withstand strong ocean winds and currents, the human hand could easily cause damage.

I was scared at first, I hadn't spent much time in the ocean, but I was also excited! With trepidation I lowered my body into the river and put my snorkeling mask on. The first time I put my face in the water and saw the miraculous world that awaited, my fear turned to wonder. The water was clear as far as the eye could see in every direction, including below us. Perhaps the most exhilarating moment was when I swam directly over a large stingray who had buried itself in the sandy sea floor. It appeared to be waking up and shaking the sand off himself just as I swam over, I was terrified if also awe struck.

While the days offered experiences I had only dreamed about, at the end of every fabulous day was a dinner I began to dread. It was evident by day three that the systematic raping of my mother's dignity would begin by five o'clock. She couldn't resist the alcohol and would quickly get drunk; it was as though a veil came over her, changing her eyes. Cody and Chad expected this and even encouraged it, singing her happy birthday at every restaurant, garnering more drinks and attention until she passed out, face first in her food.

Once I made this recognition, the rest of the trip, while

still very special, was tainted by the inevitable evening spectacle. I also started noticing how Cody was speaking to her throughout the day, quietly shaming her or giving her a compliment followed by a dig. Someone might not notice if they weren't paying attention...but I did. It had been seven months since we last saw them and something had definitely shifted. Cody wasn't as warm as he had been at the wedding, he wasn't a jerk, but something was definitely off.

A True Love Story

By my third year in school, it was clear that my marriage to Ripley wasn't going to work. It was customary to practice various healing modalities with our peers in class and as such we all went through our own transformational healing journey. It is common that when healing old wounds, some relationships that once served, become intolerable and fall away. This could mean friendships, partnerships or even work relationships; for me it meant that Ripley and I were bound to split. It was impossible for me to get comfortable with this idea even though I knew it was the right thing to do, luckily... *God had a plan to help push me along.*

I met Doug in Chicago when he came into Uncle Dan's, the outdoor store where I was working at the time. He was petting Charlie when our eyes first met.

"Great dog, what's his name?" he said looking up with kind blue eyes.

"Charlie." I replied, lovingly looking at Charlie.

"Is he yours?"

"We are each other's. Can I help you find anything?"

"Yeah, uh…. I am heading to Switzerland for the new year, and I need some long underwear."

It was the turn of the century, December 1999 and he shared how he planned to be sledding in the Alps to ring in the New Year.

We effortlessly hit it off, he was easy to talk to and we held eye contact naturally. I saw kindness in his eyes and a kindred mountain soul...*he felt comforting.* No one I knew in the city understood nature the way I did, even here, working in this outdoor store, but I could feel that essence in him and I think he felt something in me too.

"You must be from Colorado or Montana," I say after just meeting him. "I just can't peg you for a city boy." I think that one line stole his heart...*I had seen him!*

Doug's eyes, already a beautiful blue, lit up as he smiled in recognition, "Yeah, I mean I lived in Montana for a few years and Telluride for a season, I love the mountains!"

"I am from Colorado myself, Vail." Bending down to pet Charlie and without breaking eye contact, I ask, "What brings you to the city, then?"

"I work for an adventure travel company based here, but I spend the summers guiding bicycle trips throughout Europe." That sounded cool and he knew it.

I stood back up, "That sounds fun, let me show you our long underwear." We wandered over to the long underwear section and took some time debating wool versus polyester before he decided on a pair.

"So, what's the best part of traveling through Europe?" I continue the conversation.

"It's an awesome pedal powered dream through European history. The biking is great, and the different cultures are amazing but what truly stands out are the people you meet along the way, don't let them fool you, people are pretty amazing if you let them be," he says with a smile before continuing on. "Every country is unique in its own way but my favorite place to be right now is probably France, from the ocean to the mountains and the countryside in-between, it is all pretty great...*but also lonely at times*," he says as he loses focus for a second. "Oh wait, sorry, what do you do? I mean, you work here of course," he says, a little flustered. He had done the thing that people tended to do with me which is share more information than they normally feel comfortable with, but he caught it, stumbled a little, but we moved on.

"Actually, I am studying Chinese Medicine."

"Oh wow, that's cool, like acupuncture?"

"Kinda, just like there are different areas of study in western medicine, there are different branches of study in Chinese Medicine, acupuncture is just one branch. I focus more on the emotional and spiritual branch."

"Oh." he gives a typical response; people don't know what to do with this information.

We had been talking for quite some time and it was clearly time to let him go, so I processed his purchase and off he went to Switzerland.

I thought that was the last I'd see of him until about a week later, when a postcard from Switzerland showed up at Uncle Dan's, addressed to *"**Colorado Girl**"* from *"**Montana Boy**."* The postcard was a picture of a single cow standing next to a road sign at the top of a mountain pass in the Swiss Alps.

The message read:

"Hello Colorado girl, Greetings from Switzerland!!! Never caught your name when I was in a rush buying long-underwear before I left but just wanted to drop a "hello" to tell you how beautiful it is out here. Our brief chat had my mind reminiscing to hikes in Colorado and backcountry skiing in Montana. So now you know Swiss matches up and here in Grindelwald they even have a large Japanese tourist population which is longing for Japanese medicine. Anyway, hope you had a wonderful New Year and Chicago is hanging in there. Went sledding for 8 miles with 6 different nationalities at midnight to celebrate and danced all night in the streets of Grindelwald. Happy New Year and hope to talk to you again when back in Chicago.

Chow,

Doug aka "Montana Boy"

I didn't give much thought to this postcard; it was not the first time something like this had happened. In truth, I hardly remembered him. I had sold backpacks, tents, and hiking boots to many who sent their thanks through a postcard to Uncle Dan's, most of them men. I think that they mistook my genuine interest in their adventure and desire to make sure they were prepared as other interests. I was married to Ripley at the time, so I felt grateful I was of service to these folks and let it go. The postcard senders rarely showed back up, but Doug did...*he kept showing up!*

When Doug came to the store to see me, he would buy small things; socks, books, or a t-shirt to disguise his intentions. He even came a few times looking for me when I wasn't there, my friends and co-workers thought he might be a stalker, but I had zero concern. I had more concern that he always showed up to Uncle Dan's super sweaty, it was kind of gross.

Later I learned Doug used his bike as his primary mode of transportation, which meant he was sweaty from riding hard through the city. That changed his sweaty condition from gross to hot.

Doug kept popping in to see me and without too much effort we became genuine friends. During one interaction, still at Uncle Dan's, I shared with him that I had a partner (this was the fad word at the time for more than a girlfriend) and that we were having challenges. He only showed a slight WTF expression before buying a book called *Barefoot Hiking with Children* that he said was for his sister and then left.

After about a month of this, we finally exchanged numbers and began getting together to play backgammon and go for walks with Charlie. We would also try to find decent weed for each other, something we both found unnecessarily hard in Chicago after living in mountain towns. We were friends; it was easy, and I found him comforting.

During the time Doug and I were becoming friends, my wife Ripley and I were separating. The breakup didn't necessarily have anything to do with Doug, except that Doug is my soulmate, so it did. The breakup with Ripley was a long time coming, I didn't know that Doug was my soulmate at the time. I was breaking up with Ripley mostly because we just weren't nice to each other anymore.

By the spring of 2000, Ripley had moved out but still had some personal items as well her cat, Sammy, at what had been our place. I was getting ready to go out to meet a friend one night when Ripley showed up. By this point she had spit on me, thrown things at me and called me lots of names, but I always took it. I wouldn't say I took the high road; I would just say that I took it, and that night Ripley wouldn't let up. I just wanted to get out of there, but she kept going, trying to get me to engage, she wanted a fight. I could feel my temper starting to rise, I knew it very well might get the best of me, so I began deep breathing and walked away from her when, **BAM!** She threw my heavy snow boot at me. That was it, I stormed over to her, picked her up and held her against the wall by her shoulders, her feet not touching the ground.

"That's enough Ripley, I don't want to do this anymore, do you understand me?" She looked at me like a deer in headlights, she hadn't seen me lose my temper before. "I am fucking serious! I have had enough, no more name calling, you will not throw things at me, you will get your stuff and your cat, and you will leave, do you understand!" I am still holding her up against the wall.

"I don't have anywhere for Sammy to go." She was scared but she loved that cat more than anything and she was serious, she needed me.

"You have one week to find a place for Sammy, now get the fuck out of here!"

My adrenaline was pumping, I was jacked! "Jesus, I can't believe her, who throws things at someone's head, fucking psycho!" I had to talk myself down before I went out to meet my friend Rachel for a few drinks at The Crazy Horse.

The Crazy Horse is a strip club in Chicago where an ex-girlfriend and now good friend, Rachel frequented. She knew most of the strippers by name and they were all quite friendly with her. Just before I left the house, for some reason, I called Doug and asked him to join us, I knew Rachel wouldn't mind. I am not sure if he knew what it was, but he said he would meet us there.

In true form, Doug rode his bike to the strip club. When he asked the valet to park it, they just laughed at him, so he chained it to a nearby fence hoping it wouldn't get stolen.

This might be a good time to fill you in a little on who Doug is as a person, though I imagine you have some idea already. Doug is an athlete, an adventure seeker, a musician and a romantic, but above all else, Doug is kind. I don't know that he would ever choose to go to a strip club on his own, but with a bizarre invitation from me, he couldn't pass it up.

Doug found Rachel and I at a small round table in the middle of the club. He was wearing a button-down shirt and pants, his right pant leg still rolled up from riding his bike and he had a messenger bag slung over his shoulder. It was one of the first times I saw him when he didn't appear to be sweaty.

As an aside, how sweet is it that Doug dressed up to go to a strip club?!

We had a great view of the main stage and were surrounded by several small stages as well. As the girls got done with their act, they would come join us and chat, mostly with Rachel. They faked "hellos" to us but seemed to have some deep connection or allegiance to her. For Rachel, it was par for the course, she had a way about her. She used to tell me when she got lap dances, she would just look the girls in the eyes the whole time, never looking at their bodies, "It makes them feel special, more connected, that's why they all hang out with me."

This was the second or third time I had been to The Crazy Horse with Rachel. We were both going through a breakup, and this was just sort of how we were coping. We were always the only two women in the place with clothes on. I don't know why I was there; I wasn't really into strippers; it was more of a distraction than anything I suppose.

I was just getting ready to buy a lap dance for Doug when Rachel whispered something in a stripper's ear. The song that came next was *Honky Tonk Women by The Rolling Stones*. I looked over at Doug, expecting to see a surprised and uncomfortable look on his face only to see "Bunny" shaking her boobs in my face while grinding on Doug. She continued the two-way lap dance between Doug and I for the entire song. I am not sure if Doug was able to enjoy it or if he was uncomfortable but to this day, *Honky Tonk Women* is still our song.

Nothing happened between Doug and I after that night at the Crazy Horse. We remained friends, played backgammon together and listened to music. He even hung with my dog Charlie when I went out of town, but there wasn't a romantic connection, more like a kinship.

The Last Leg

As part of the 800-hr Chinese Medicine program, I was expected to complete an additional 100 hours of practicum (supervised practice, otherwise understood as an internship). I chose to divide it between my Points and Channels teacher, Dr. Le Roy, who had a busy practice as a Chiropractic Internist in downtown Chicago and Renee Ryan, my Jin Shin Do® Authorized Teacher® who had an office in the suburbs called, *The Light Heart Center.*

Each internship gave me invaluable knowledge toward the inner workings of the business I wanted to create. They taught me both how much I knew and how much I still had to learn.

Dr. Le Roy's office demonstrated a beautiful blend between Western and Eastern medicine creating a balanced approach to health and healing. He was on the cutting edge of advanced healthcare, and I was exposed to some of the first Thermography technology and the myriad of ways in which to use it to find all types of precancerous conditions. I did my first pap smear and breast exam in this office as well, which wasn't really what I was there for, but I found it fascinating.

Dr. Le Roy was a total brainiac, incredibly intelligent and well-studied. While I respected him tremendously, I knew I wasn't going to go to medical school as he did, nor was it my nature to run a busy downtown clinic out of a high rise while wearing a white lab coat. That said, it was an incredible experience, and I learned a ton of practical knowledge that I still use today.

After I had completed my first fifty hours with Dr. Le Roy, I ventured to the suburbs to work with Renee, at *The Light Heart Center.* Days spent here were full of love and unity.

Renee offered a lunch time Qi Gong class in a practice known as Eight Pieces of Silk. Instead of charging admission, she requested a canned food donation that she would then give to the local food pantry. She was committed to her service and a true role model for me.

The Light Heart Center is where I felt most at home. The clientele sought a safe space to move through emotional hurt and Renee's office offered just that, a warm space full of plants with light pouring in from the south facing windows most of the day. It was painted soft blue and trimmed in warm wood tones creating a peaceful atmosphere. I related much more to this feel than that of Dr. Le Roy's office, though both are very much necessary.

I worked with Renee and her clients under her supervision for about two months before she asked me to work with her directly as is required by The Jin Shin Do® Foundation to ensure my readiness. The sessions were beautiful, I had the same effect on her as I did my peers and without hesitation, she told me I was ready.

This type of work is my gift, and I am forever grateful to the Divine intervention that brought me to school and to my incredible teacher of four years, Renee. She saw my gifts and really helped me develop them beyond modality, she helped me remember how to listen and guided me home to my true nature.

The Vision

While finishing my practicum hours at *The Light Heart Center*, Steve, a hypnotherapist, and psychologist who also worked there, told me of a man named John of God. John of God was a world-renowned healer and medium working out of a healing center in Brazil and Steve thought I might be interested in joining a group he was leading down there the following month.

The timing felt perfect, I needed to get out of the city and process my divorce from Ripley. My hours at The Light Heart Center would be fulfilled by then so all that was left was finding a place for Charlie, which of course turned out to be with Doug. Doug and Charlie were like two peas in a pod, both of them would be better for the time spent together.

After a twelve-hour flight and very little food, I was tired and grumpy when we landed in Brazil. I had a hard time orienting at first, perhaps because I had crossed the equator. However, I also wasn't comfortable being so closely tied to eleven other people I didn't know; some of whom felt scattered, desperate, and even fanatical. They seemed to believe John of God was going to completely heal them of anything and everything. It made me uncomfortable giving this one man so much power, but I was there; I was seeking something, a knowing in myself perhaps more than anything else, so I did my best to trust the process.

Once the plane landed, we had a two-hour bus ride to the town of Abanjania, where the healing center that John of God served was located. We stayed in a simple fifteen room hotel with a small dining hall. The hotel was unique at the time in that it had both running water and hot showers.

Abanjania was a third world town where chickens and dogs roamed the streets only to be plucked off for a meal the next day. It was a place where kids played soccer with a newspaper stuffed sock for a ball and where clean running water was hard to come by.

This tiny town was put on the map solely because of John of God. It was struggling to meet its own needs when the demands of "spiritual tourism" put added pressure on it. For those who were able to see the opportunity, things were quite good but much of the town was still struggling to survive.

John Of God is an everyday man who also happens to be a medium. A medium is someone who can surrender their body and mind to be an open vessel or clear channel for those in the spirit world to move through. John of God is said to be a channel for several saints, archangels, and healers.

We walked a wide red dirt road from our hotel to the healing center every morning, passing rows of broken houses, occasionally seeing a new, well-built two-story house; the home of someone who was able to harness the new economy. We passed a dilapidated brick factory surrounded by old bricks with large smokestacks still towering into the sky, a faint chemical smell lingered in the air. All in all, it was a little over a half mile from our hotel to the healing center and along the way, others joined the walk coming from their own accommodations. By the time we reached the center, there might have been a hundred people walking with us.

The mornings often started with a show and tell experience where John of God would do a physical surgery with no anesthesia, pulling something awful out of someone's brain through their nose. This was no doubt to convince us to have unwavering trust in him. For me, it was a spectacle and only furthered my initial distrust of him. What he was doing was real, I saw it with my own eyes time and time again, he was pulling cancer right out of people through their skin, it was truly incredible! That said, someone of the light has no need to prove their worth and convince you of their gifts. I found John of God's display to be that of someone still working with ego and perhaps not entirely of the light...or perhaps, I have a hard time trusting anyone in authority.

Once the demonstration was over, we all shuffled over to the entrance that led to John of God's healing room. The protocol was this; you wrote on a piece of paper what you were seeking, then stand in a single file line in the sweltering heat until you reach John of God. He is sitting in a simple chair with an interpreter/guide on either side of him. You hand the paper to one of the interpreters who reads it and then passes it on to John of God. He is able to read it no matter what language it is written in. John of God may then ask a question but generally just directs you to either sit "in current" in the meditation room or the spiritual surgery room. In either room you sit in current or meditation for hours, but it is believed that in the spiritual surgery room, surgery is actually being done on you while you meditate.

This four-hour long experience ends with a community meal of soup and crystal water. The soup is the only meal served at the healing center and is the same every day. They must make it by the tens of gallons, every pilgrim or seeker eats this soup after their first four hours of sitting in current. The crystal water is said to come from a spring that passes through a reservoir of rose quartz that the healing center sits on.

I couldn't get comfortable at the healing center, though I wasn't able to pinpoint why, I found I wasn't the only one. One of my group members was talking about how there was Reptilian energy all around and under the healing center and he could feel the insidious shadow of the place. He was convinced John of God was Reptilian and breeding with the women around him to create more Reptilians on the planet. I didn't really know what the fuck he was talking about, but I listened just the same, trying to discern the truth while staying grounded. After such an intense and bizarre conversation, I welcomed the evening dinner and swing dancing that came after.

Never in my life have I had more joyful fun than when I was swing dancing with a "pro" down in Brazil. All I had to do was follow his movements and let go, he had me rolling over his back, scooting under his legs and twirling all over the dance floor, it was an hour of pure bliss!

The second day at the healing center, I gave John of God my piece of paper; I can't remember what it said, but it probably had something to do with being whole and feeling worthy of love. As with each person before me, he told me to sit in current. Annoyed that's all I got from him, I joined the other pilgrims and sat on a hard bench in a dingy hot room. Light poured in through the open windows illuminating the dust particles in the air as I attempted to meditate.

The people sitting around me were crying, rocking back and forth, moaning, and praying. I sat there frustrated, watching everyone else move through their process while I quite notably felt nothing. Sitting in current refers to the collective energy flow we share as we sit together meditating and how that collective flow amplifies the healing energy or "current."

It took me a while to settle in but when I finally dropped

into meditation I saw a pregnant woman, she was walking along the river holding someone's hand. In the beginning of the meditation, I could only see the back of the woman, when I asked to see who I was watching, it was revealed to be me. When I looked over to see whose hand I was holding, it was Doug.

Of course it was Doug, it has always been Doug, from the first time we met...Julie, an Uncle Dan's co-worker and friend knew it when I tried to set her up with him, my ex-wife knew it as soon as I said his name, Rachel knew it when she set up that double lap dance and Doug knew it, Doug knew it from the first time our eyes met.

The next day I went into "town" to get a calling card so I could use the one pay phone in a hundred-mile radius to call him. I spent $40 for a five-minute call which he thankfully answered. This was long before cell phones and I didn't know what time it was in Chicago or what he would be doing, but he answered.

After I said hello, I almost couldn't say anything else, I mean I knew what I wanted to say, but I almost couldn't admit it out loud. So, the conversation sounded something like this:

Me: "Um, hi."

Doug: "Hi! How are you doing? Is it amazing over there?"

Me: "Um, yeah, um there is something I want to tell you, it's just I don't, um...um it's just that I think. Um...well I think I... do you know what I am trying to say?"

Doug: "No, not really, can you give me something to go on?"

Me: "Never mind, how is Charlie?"

Doug: "Charlie is great, I love Charlie, we are having a great time. What's up Jess?"

Me: "Well, it's just, I am like here, you know and well, um I had to sit in current for like four hours and I kind of realized something and um...it's just that well, you know...I don't know."

Doug: "Jess, what are you talking about?"

Me: "I just think like maybe I, well we are kind of, I mean I think like we are supposed to you know, it's just. What do you think? Do you understand what I am trying to say?"

Doug: *silence*

Doug: "Um, well, I don't know, maybe. I mean I think so, but I don't want to be wrong about this."

Me: "Oh no! You are not wrong, it's just, oh shit I am almost out of time here, ok, you have my flight info, yes? You will pick me up from the airport, right? Oh my God, I have to go. Wait, are you ok?"

Doug: "Um, I don't know, wait, yes I have your flight info, um I will pick you up. So, I will see you soon?"

Me: "Ok, thanks, ok, bye."

Doug: "Bye?"

That awkward phone conversation was the start of it all.

The rest of my time visiting Abenjania was spent learning and observing. I met some interesting teachers including a tantric healer who told me my grandmother was *The Keeper of The Tree to The Soul of The Earth,* something that resonated deeply with my heart and explained my draw to trees and nature.

It felt safe to tell her about my experience in current and how it didn't make any sense because I was a lesbian. She laughed with delight as she told me she could see the cords Doug and I shared, she told me not to fight it because it was meant to be... then she had to explain to me what cords were.

Cords are energetic ties or "cords" that connect us. Parents and children share cords, friends and lovers share cords, sometimes we have cords tethered to past lives and some cords can bind us in unhealthy situations or keep us stuck in our trauma. I could write a chapter on these things but suffice it to say, Doug and I shared magical cords, connecting our hearts with incredible light.

Purge Pots

Steve, our group leader, organized an outing for us to watch a sacred Ayahuasca ceremony with an ancient tribe of the area (long before it became the "cool thing" to do in Western culture). I wasn't sure what Ayahuasca was, but even before we left, I felt like the journey ahead was not in alignment and I was hesitant to go.

Nevertheless, we piled into villagers' cars and drove about five miles to the edge of the jungle, then walked a dirt footpath to a small clearing where a colorful canopy marked the ceremony site. It was clear as we arrived that some of the tribe's people were uncomfortable to have us there.

In theory, Ayahuasca is a sacred plant medicine coupled with ceremony meant to help you connect with God and heal your soul. *Can you imagine trying to do that while a bunch of strangers watched? I would be uncomfortable too!*

The tribe was already seated, men and women separated

but facing each other. Each person had a hand carved pot ordained with what looked like gold. Once we found our seats behind the women, the High Priest spoke in his native language, signaling it was time to begin. There was very little chanting or ceremony to it that we were privileged to, perhaps they had done something before we came but what we saw was uneventful. The Priest took a drink of Ayahuasca Tea from a large goblet and then passed the goblet to the man on his left. Each man in turn would take his drink and pass it on, there were two rows with twelve people each, so it took quite some time. When the men were done, the Priest collected the goblet and refilled it before handing it to the women on his right.

Soon, we could see and feel the Ayahuasca take hold, the first men that drank it began to rock back and forth while others were spinning from their waist. Their legs began to move, almost like they were anxious and then they would reach for their gold ordained pot and... purge.

The tribe's people were not allowed to move from their seats, even to puke, so we had the distinct privilege of watching several people puke, poop, and pee all over themselves and then have to sit in it for the remainder of the ceremony.

We were all horrified and realized as soon as it all began that we had no business being there, unfortunately we were also not allowed to leave our seats for any reason, so we had to sit there the entire four hours.

After sitting in the Brazilian rainforest for four hours dealing with bugs the size of my fist, we were desperate to get out of there. It was dark by the time it was over, but we managed ok on the footpath heading out to the parking area where we would meet our drivers. As we approached, we saw the parking area had become a giant festival complete with food vendors and crafts. It seemed the whole town came out to celebrate after the ceremony. We were totally blindsided and not at all excited about this new development. All twelve of us in the group were ready to get back to our rooms and put this day to rest, unfortunately we had to endure another hour of "celebration" before we convinced the villagers to give us a ride back to our accommodations.

The Long Way Home

I was ready to leave Brazil long before our trip was scheduled to be over, once I had admitted to myself that Doug was my soul mate, I only wanted to get to him. We hadn't spoken since that one awkward phone conversation and didn't talk again until my plane landed in Miami, seven days later. Our connecting flight to Chicago had been canceled and I was heartbroken. The first thing I did when I arrived in my hotel room was pick up the phone and call Doug.

I don't remember the exact conversation word for word, but I know I was frustrated, tired, and wanted to see him. The part I do remember is when he said, "cheer up buttercup" and my heart melted. We still didn't directly address the "elephant in the room," but we both felt it in our hearts, and I realized in that moment that I had been waiting my whole life to meet this man.

I was nervous as the plane descended into Chicago, I had no idea what my expectations were or even how I would react to

Doug, but my body was vibrating in anticipation.

Doug was waiting for me at the gate when I exited the jetway, his face beaming with light, yet clearly just as nervous as I was. We were awkward and lost in each other all at the same time, so much so that Doug lost the car, and we traipse around parking lots for thirty minutes trying to find it.

We only had three months together before his planned move from Chicago to Colorado for a job he had already committed to. I still had a year of school left so our relationship was destined to continue the way it started, long distance.

I wish I could say everything was easy peasy from there, but there were many bumps, mostly mine. One moment I felt safe and perfect in his arms, the next confused. I had just spent eight years convincing my parents that my being a lesbian wasn't a phase...it was difficult to reconcile.

Needless to say, Doug put up with some shit while I figured mine out, most notably when he flew to Chicago for a surprise visit. As the visit progressed, I was having to introduce him to people as my boyfriend which made me feel terribly awkward, even though nobody cared I wasn't a lesbian but me. At some point, my level of bitchiness and ridiculousness hit a peak, and Doug said he needed some space from me and was going to go for a walk.

That man walked himself out the door, got on a train straight to the airport and flew home. After a few hours, I called his friends that we were supposed to meet up with for dinner to see if they knew where he was, they didn't. Then he called me, from back in Colorado.

That rocked me to my core, I was hurt, angry, confused and honestly...*impressed*. I was awful to this man while I was trying to get my own shit sorted out and I was sure he was going to take it. I didn't think he had a backbone which as anyone knows is very unattractive, however, that single act sent the message, you will not treat me this way and I never took him for granted again.

In the phone conversation that followed, he told me he loved me more than anything, but he wasn't going to be treated like dirt. He would wait a while for me to figure it out, but not forever. I am pretty sure I understood in that moment what I may have lost, and I apologized.

Chapter Thirteen

The End of an Empire

By now, our fur stores had been paired down to accommodate a change in culture. The decade of excess that accompanied the eighties gave way to a more conservative culture in the nineties and with a rise in animal rights protests, fur became slightly less desirable. Luckily our smart business decisions meant we were still making money hand over fist; the wealthy didn't give a shit about the activism.

The business of breeding and showing horses was also thriving. Both my mom and Hillis spent winters working their asses off in Vail but retired to their ranches to work with horses for the off-season months. By this time, they were confident in their long-term employees who kept the stores running through the summers.

Hillis' nature was to find an angle...any angle that made him more money. After getting lucky in both the fur and horse industries he felt ready to play with the big boys. Through various connections, he caught wind of a new opportunity in the *"high-end"* European auto trade. He had met a group of men who claimed to be bringing luxury cars into the United States for established clientele at a great profit margin. Of course he saw this as his next move and blindly invested $100,000 of company money without discussion or consideration of my mother or the business obligations that needed to be met.

Hillis lost every penny; he had been scammed.

My mom knew Hillis had always skimmed cash off the top, it was just built into the system, but this time it was too much. He clearly had no regard for her, our family, or the business they had built together. She finally had enough.

Court battles ensued, on one side was a cornered animal and on the other, the man that beat that animal into the corner. My mother, to her credit, stood strong against his tactics of intimidation and blame. She fought for what she believed she earned and despite desperately wanting love and approval from her father, she stood up for herself and she won.

The win of course was bittersweet, her father would never speak to her again, except once when he needed to borrow money, which he has never paid back.

This isn't what she wanted, she wanted a kind father that wanted to take care of her, she wanted him to see her as valuable simply because she existed, she wanted her dad.

My mother continued to run the business, eventually pairing down the stores again. She lost one of her buildings and consequently a store in her divorce from David but continued to run one Aspen and one Vail store for several more years.

That's all that is left of a once thriving empire. An empire that gave me a good life, paid for my education, and helped me buy my first house. An empire that tore my family apart and used everyone in it like a pawn to cultivate more money for a tyrant.

To this day, my mother, who can no longer form many words intentionally, can tell you that what she misses most about her life is working with her dad. Even after how he treated her and her siblings, after all the degradation and withholding, after all the money he took... the thing she misses most about her life is running that company with her father. I find that to be extraordinary.

Chapter Fourteen

Gun with a Silencer

I graduated on September 22, 2001, just eleven days after 9/11. Although I was the first one to graduate from college in my family, no one was willing to travel to see me or celebrate, no one except Doug. He took four days off work and drove fourteen hours to celebrate and honor my hard work. Even though I understood why people didn't want to travel, it was hard not to have my family there. I again felt "not good enough" or like they didn't take my education in Chinese Medicine seriously. That was my baggage, but it still hurt.

It was time to leave Chicago again, this time I knew it would be for good. Chicago had given me a great deal; my first true friendships and the ability to explore diversity, both in people and culture but also within myself. It gave me my best friend and savior; Charlie and it gave me an education and foundation I could develop into a career. Chicago was the unlikely place that two mountain souls found each other, and it is where I will finally leave feeling I completed my journey, grateful for all it offered me. My heart was calling me back to the mountains, back to Doug.

After I graduated, I moved to my mom's ranch in Eagle and stayed in an attached bedroom outside of the main house for about a month. By this time, she and Cody had been together about two years, I didn't want to stay in the house and cramp their style. From what I could tell, their relationship had morphed into an isolated world of paranoia and partying, and I didn't want any part of that.

While I was living in Chicago, I hadn't known how my mom and Cody's relationship was going, she always implied it was great, but when I got there, it was clear something strange was going on. One afternoon while I was making lunch in the main house, Cody stopped me for a conversation.

"Hey Jess, if you hear a gun go off in the middle of the night, that's just me chasing people away ok." Cody had pulled me outside, out of earshot of my mom.

"What people Cody, no one is out there trying to get us." I say, obviously condescending, though I didn't mean to be.

"Hasn't your mom told you what's been going on? Someone stole her horse trailer, we found it on the side of the road up near Edwards." He wouldn't look me in the eyes.

"That doesn't make any sense Cody, who steals something only to leave it on the side of the road, not to mention, it takes time to steal a horse trailer, you have to hook it up. There is no way the dogs didn't notice or that you didn't notice, you guys notice every car that drives down here. What the fuck is going on?"

"Look Jess, I don't know what to tell you, some strange shit has been happening in this neck of the woods, you haven't been around in a while. See here that's why I got this silencer, then it won't wake anyone up if I have to fire it in the middle of the night." Cody shows me a large gun with what he says is a silencer on it.

"You just told me that I might hear you shooting in the middle of the night and not to be scared, but if you have a silencer, I wouldn't hear it anyway, right?" I had no idea what Cody was trying to do, he wasn't making sense. Was he trying to scare me under the guise of protecting me?

"Now Jessica, I am telling you to be careful around here, you hear... That's it."

"Yeah, Ok Cody. Are you alright man, you seem a little jittery."

"Oh yeah, I am good, I am real good."

Later that same day, Doug came over from Carbondale to spend the night. He was in the main house talking with my mom when he spotted Cody's gun with the silencer resting on the countertop, he was floored. He left the conversation with my mom and came to find me in my room.

"Jess, there is a gun on the kitchen counter." Doug looked like a deer in headlights.

"That sounds about right, did it have a silencer on it?" I say nonchalantly.

"What? I don't know, why is there a gun on the kitchen counter?" He is clearly out of his depth here.

"I don't know, Cody says there are people around trying to steal from my mom, but I think he is full of shit." I am not particularly concerned and continue folding laundry as we are talking.

"Doesn't it bother you that there are guns just out like that?" Doug's words are drawn out.

"Oh, I don't know babe, it's kind of par for the course around here, it's a ranch."

"Do you feel safe?" Doug was clearly uncomfortable.

"I mean, I guess--what's up love, you seem anxious."

"I can't be here knowing there is a loaded gun on the counter, I mean, knowing that guns may be shot near or around me doesn't feel safe. Let's go to my house." He was looking around now as though a gun might go off at any moment.

"Ok, yeah babe, I am sorry this is so weird for you, I kind of just skipped over it, but yeah, you're right, it's fucked up…. I just need to bring Charlie."

Life at the ranch was getting stranger by the day and I left the ranch for good soon after. I think Cody and my mom were doing meth together and he was getting her paranoid on purpose in order to control her. From the time I left, things just became weirder and weirder.

I learned that Cody was feeding my mom drugs nonstop and had even forced some on my brother. I also caught him poisoning our German Shepherd, Cruiser, by intentionally putting a leak in his radiator and letting the antifreeze seep out. He was out of control.

About six months after I had moved out, Doug and I

stopped by the ranch one afternoon unannounced on our way to a nearby hike and found my mom inside with all the curtains closed and the house sealed up tight on a beautiful spring day. She was skinny as fuck with scabs all over her face, no light in her eyes but talking a mile a minute, trying to cover up the fact that she was high. It was sickening.

After being there a few minutes, we noticed there were wires hanging out of the wall and small burn marks on the wood walls of her log home. I had lived there only a few months ago, I couldn't believe how quickly the situation had deteriorated.

"Mom, what happened with all these wires? Why are they sticking out of the wall?"

"Oh Jessica, they are spying on us, we had to disconnect everything because they are listening to us through the speakers." My mom had grave concern on her face, I could tell she really believed what she was saying.

"Mom, what are you talking about, why would anyone spy on you? All you do is watch TV, ride horses and go to work."

Cody stepped in and handed me a small square shaped piece of black plastic with a clear lens in it. "Look at this, we found this camera hidden in the walls."

"That is the lens to a CD reader." Doug said flatly, "I see the CD player has been taken apart, was that you Cody?" Doug looked Cody directly in the eyes, calling him out.

"Hey Cody, how about you and I go for a walk." I said, motioning to the back door.

"Yeah, sure, ok, let's go." He was doubling down.

I walked him out to the garage, "I know what you are doing, and I am going to call the police."

"Oh yeah, the police, what are you going to tell them, that your mom is an addict? I am clean, you got nothing on me." He was looking me in the eyes now and had a smirk on his face.

My only option was to evoke emotion, "Cody, you love her, you became part of our family, why are you doing this?"

"I ain't doing nothing Jessica." He had glee in his eyes, he knew he was winning this battle.

He was right, there was nothing I could do and if anyone got in trouble it would be my mom. There was no use talking to Cody anymore and talking to my mom wasn't going to work in the state she was in, so I went back to the house, grabbed Doug and left; sad, confused, and angry.

Chapter Fifteen

Crack Christmas

The first Christmas I spent with my mom once I moved back to Colorado was a vibrant reminder of why being around my mom was so unpredictable. She had finally broken up with Cody after a particularly bad trip to Mexico, though she did not elaborate on what that meant, and insisted on claiming her freedom by throwing a Christmas party for all those who had nowhere else to go. Doug and I agreed to attend in support of her getting away from Cody, though admittedly we were both a little nervous.

We arrived at what seemed like a normal Christmas dinner, there were a few friendly faces, including my brother, Chad but most people were new to us. Christmas music was playing, and decorations were all around, but it didn't take long to notice something was off. No one was able to hold a conversation and they kept disappearing in groups of three for up to ten minutes at a time.

When the turkey came out of the oven, as many as ten people gathered around it while they watched in awe as Gene, my mom's neighbor, and drug dealer I later found out, melted four sticks of butter on top of it.

We knew all these behaviors implied drug use, but it didn't follow the norms for weed or for cocaine and we couldn't quite recognize the high.

When dinner was served, everyone made huge plates of food, but no one sat down to eat any of it, instead they kept going outside. At one point after dinner, just as we all gathered in the living room in front of the fire to open gifts, every person there disappeared. Doug and I were left alone, wondering where they all went when I made the joke, "*What are they all on, crack!?*" And right then, we knew, yes, they were actually smoking crack in the room that I used to stay in. We sat there and awaited their return, not really knowing what to do or how to process this new information...*I mean, Crack on Christmas, come on!*

When everyone came back to the room, it was clear they were indeed on crack and sure enough, a super inappropriate conversation ensued. Things I didn't want to know about my brother's sex life, my mom's sex life, and the sex lives of others in the room. It was clear in that moment; the drug use did not stop when Cody moved out. Doug and I looked at each other and decided to get the hell out of there and I haven't spent a Christmas at my mom's house since.

It wasn't long after Christmas that my mom's life really spiraled out of control, the drugs kept flowing eventually causing her to both look and sound destitute. She had a long-time employee running her stores while she stayed strung out on meth or crack for months. Doug and I pretty much stayed out of her life at this point, but my brother remained and saw countless horrible things that I imagine have traumatized him to this day.

Chapter Sixteen

Bean

Before Doug and I were engaged, we got pregnant with our first child, Bean, named for his shape and size early in development. I was sick as fuck and was losing weight fast, food didn't appeal to me, but I was told time and time again, I had to find a way to eat. It seemed clear to me the best option would be to travel to Chicago, my food mecca and eat my way through the rest of my first trimester. My dear friend Julie was happy to accommodate and join me on the fabulous food extravaganza. Julie and I have this awesome relationship where we travel to be together and then eat our way through each visit. Even when I lived in Chicago, our primary connection was eating, we loved to love food together!

I had let my mom know I was traveling but she didn't yet know I was pregnant. I didn't really trust her, and I just wasn't ready to go down that road.

The first few days of my Chicago visit were wonderful! Julie and I had no problem stuffing our faces with all our favorite foods. It wasn't until day four, when I traveled to the suburbs to visit my friend Corri that things turned sideways.

Corri was a friend I made while working at Healing Earth Resources my last year of school. She was younger than me by six years but in love with a man six years my elder, who she had recently moved in with. They had been building their dream house, complete with vegetable gardens and chickens. I was so excited to see her and celebrate her new life, but for some reason I was quite agitated. After about an hour at her house, I became consumed by anger for no real reason, I was furious, spinning even and I had no idea why. The anger wasn't directed at anything or anyone, but it was big and palpable. I could name it but even after going for a walk around their sweet pond I couldn't shake it. I was unreasonably rage filled for no reason when I should have been feeling joyful for my friend.

Then, I got a call.

"Hello."

"Hi Jess, how are you?" It was Doug.

"I am ok, what's up? Why'd you track me down?" Still, I didn't have a cell phone, so Doug had to call Julie to get my whereabouts.

"There is no easy way to say this honey, um...it's about your mom."

"What about my mom?"

"Babe, she...she shot Cody today...he's dead."

There was silence while tears welled up in my eyes. I didn't know what to do or where to go, I was standing at Corri's kitchen counter, unsure of where to turn.

"Um, ok, is she ok, did he hurt her, what happened?"

"I don't know exactly; I know that she shot him in her living room during a fight and then she called 911 to get help."

"Where is she now?"

"She is in police custody, I think she is in jail, she said she pulled the trigger."

"Oh my God, but it had to be self-defense, right?"

"I don't know babe; I have the numbers of the Eagle jail where she is and the name of an officer who might be able to tell you more. Do you want that information?"

"Yes, yes, hold on, let me get a pen." I searched around for a piece of paper and a pen while crying my face off. "Ok, I am ready."

Doug proceeded to give me the name and number of who to contact before we got off the phone and we said our goodbyes.

I filled in my friend Corri on what had just happened and although I was supposed to spend the night, I asked them to take me back to the train station so I could get back to Julie's house in Chicago. I didn't know if I was going to head back to Colorado or what, but I couldn't just sit in the middle of the suburbs and do nothing.

Once I got back to Julie's I called the number for the Eagle County Sheriff's office. The story was this:

Cody had come to the ranch the morning of the shooting demanding money, he came at her in a drug-induced rage, with intent to kill, she had no choice but to kill or be killed, right there in her living room.

The fact that she had a gun with her really speaks to how she was living in extreme fear for her life. I think she was trying to pull her life together after she threw Cody out, but I don't think she ever really believed she would be free. Only she knows how bad it got, how often he beat her, injected her with drugs or emotionally berated her. What I know is she wasn't holding onto a gun in her living room because she felt safe.

All my unexplained anger now made sense. I had felt the incident unfold through unconscious connection to my mother. My anger subsided only slightly as I processed what had happened, but I was still angry she was in this situation at all.

The next day I bought a rose from a street vendor and carried it with me as I rode the bus through Chicago on my way to a friend's house. I was quietly weeping when a child sitting across from me earnestly asked, "What's wrong?"

I looked into her eyes and saw her innocence, I replied gently, "Someone I know has died."

"Is that why you have a flower?"

"Yes, in memory. Would you like it?"

"Really!?" She lit up with hope.

"Yes, I am happy to pass it on if it will bring you joy." I reached across the bus to hand her the rose.

"Miss," the girl's mother interrupted, "are you sure this is what you want?"

"Of course, ma'am." The girl reached out and took the rose.

"Thank you." She held the rose close to her nose, closed her eyes and inhaled deeply.

That small exchange took me out of anger and into a deeper feeling of love. My emotions moved from fear and suffering to love and compassion.

I can't imagine what it would feel like to kill someone, let alone someone you once loved who was now threatening to kill you and your family. I wept for my mom, for Cody and I wept for what I knew would be a terrible year to come.

I don't know if Cody made my mom a mark when he met her, I think so, but I also think that he accidentally found a home and family with her. I believe there was genuine love felt between them at least for a time. I don't know the trigger that caused things to change or if I am just being naive to think there was real love between them, but I do.

When I returned from Chicago a few days later, I went to visit my mom in jail. I brought her a bag full of candy bars, something I knew she would appreciate. She was happy to see me, but also ashamed I had to see her in there, wearing an orange jumpsuit, through a piece of glass.

"Hi mom, are you ok?" I asked in earnest.

"Jessica, you shouldn't have come."

"Mom, of course I came, how are you holding up?"

"Um, it's hard honey, but don't worry, I'm ok." She said

looking down at the table.

"I brought you some candy bars."

She looked up, sugar was as good a drug as anything, "Really! Thank you so much, oh wow, thank you."

"Yes, I got your favorites, Almond Joy, Salted Nut Roll and Hershey's with Almonds."

"You know what I like." She was touched.

There wasn't much else to say through a glass wall and a phone. I still had unasked questions but could see my mom's shame and didn't want to make it worse, we were both at a loss on what to say. After a long pause in the conversation, I decided to share our good news, "Mom, I'm pregnant." She burst into happy tears, as did I. And that was it, we had little else to share, so we said our goodbyes, both of us feeling empty and uncertain.

Losing Bean

The year that followed was perpetually traumatizing and painful. We lost our first child, Bean, he died at eleven weeks, but by week thirteen my body had not miscarried him. My midwife, Jules, kept telling me something wasn't right, that a miscarriage didn't look like this. She took me to the ER twice and both times, the ER doctors sent me home stating I was having a "standard miscarriage." Finally, Jules got me in with an OBGYN who quickly saw what was going on and put me in surgery that day.

This is a demonstration of how women and women's health is marginalized in our country. I had a licensed midwife bring me to the

ER, share her medical records and still, I was turned away. By the time I got care from a doctor, I was septic and could have easily died. I was in the hospital for eleven days after surgery trying to beat the sepsis.

My experience in the hospital was horrifying right from the beginning. My nurses couldn't find a vein for my IV and proceeded to bring in about six different colleagues to prick my arm. I had an older, more experienced nurse decide that if she just slapped my arm hard enough, she would bring my vein up. At this point, there were at least five other nurses in the room standing around watching, as if I was a mountain to conquer.

"That's enough." I say firmly as I pull my arm away and pull my sleeve down. I brought my eyes up to meet the sadistic nurse, "This is no way to be treated. Don't slap me around and think that it's okay. If you would like to get the cooperation of my body, work with it: be kind and show compassion. You will not be touching me again; all of you get out and find me someone with decent bedside manner!"

They all stood around dumbfounded for a moment, looking at each other like they were unsure what to do next.

"Please leave my room and find me someone who can give me compassionate care!" I stated it again slowly and clearly before they finally left.

It was soon determined that I needed a central line as my veins weren't large enough to support the necessary needle for fluids and meds. Once the central line was in, I was prepped for surgery.

As I laid in my hospital gown in the pre-op room behind a curtain, I heard a man come in.

"Your next patient is waiting, doctor." Came a woman's voice.

"What do we have here... 'Oh, says she is nervous about going under, poor thing...' Jesus, can you believe these people, it's not like we've been doing this for fifty years or something!"

He is full of narcissistic sarcasm.

"You know I can hear you, it is only a curtain that separates us." I say with notable agitation in my voice.

With one quick motion he slides the curtain open to reveal his tall thin body. "No, no darlin', I am just kidding around."

"Please don't call me darlin'. I would love it if my caregivers would be kind enough to help me through this. Can you please just take care of me?!" I asked in earnest, I was scared shitless.

He saw me, I got through and his demeanor changed completely. "Ok, Jessica, I've got you. Don't worry, I know what I am doing, you are going to be fine."

"Thank you." I exhale.

"Are you ready?" He looks me in the eyes and touches my arm.

"Yes."

"Count backwards from 99."

"99, 98.....97...................96............................
.....," and I was out.

Surgery had been successful, but after forty-eight hours my body wasn't responding to the broad-spectrum antibiotics my doctor insisted on.

"Hmm." my doctor said with a look of concern on his face.

"What's up?" I ask.

"Your infection isn't getting any better."

"Did you give me amoxicillin?"

"No, we need to treat you with a broad spectrum intravenous for what you have going on."

"Doctor, I told you that wasn't going to work, I told you to give me amoxicillin. Why aren't you listening to me?"

"Because I am the doctor, but we have to do something. Okay, I am going to listen to you."

He made some notes on his pad and left. A short time later the nurse came in to change my medicine and hang a new IV bag. By two o'clock the same day, I could feel a shift; the amoxicillin was working.

Doug was with me as often as possible, but still had a job and Charlie to take care of. He would sometimes spend the night if he could find care for Charlie, but that was hard on him, so I suggested he sleep at home.

We spent those first few nights playing backgammon and listening to the Ryan Adams album, Demolition, it had just come out and it served as the soundtrack for the eleven days I was in the hospital.

On one such night, a nurse came in to switch out my IV bag and as she changed the line, she created an air bubble. I knew an air bubble could be dangerous if it got into my blood stream, so I got a little nervous. She kept trying to push it out and reconnect the line successfully, but with no luck.

"Perhaps you should grab another nurse to help you." I said nervously as I watched her fumble.

"No, I got it, don't worry." she says as the air bubble is now only inches from entering my body.

"You don't 'got' it, please go get someone else." I say more firmly. She doesn't move, instead she keeps trying to push the air bubble out.

Now Doug speaks up, "Miss, I think it's time you get some help, we are running out of time here."

My stress level was at an all-time high, I clearly could not trust this woman and she still wouldn't get help, I was so tense I thought I might punch her. I just kept looking at Doug to go get someone, ready to pull the line out myself if I had to.

"Ok, I guess I will go get some help, I will be right back." She said reluctantly.

"Fuck, this lady is going to fucking kill me! How the hell am I supposed to get better under these conditions?"

"I know babe, this is scary, where's the bubble now?" Doug asked.

"It's right fucking here." I say pointing to the line, it's about two inches from entering my body.

"I am going to have to pull this fucking line out myself, just to save my own life; if this gets to my heart, I could die!"

The nurse came back with a needle, but no one else was

with her to help. She started poking at the air bubble with the needle through the line.

"What are you doing, this doesn't seem right!" I was starting to panic.

"Yeah, this is how we get rid of air bubbles, don't worry." But I was very worried, but then she got it, she popped the bubble and in disbelief, I exhaled. "See, no worries. Do you need anything else?" She asked with a smile on her face.

I just stared at her still in disbelief. She didn't even realize the stress she had caused us...was this common? "No, thank you, I think we just want to be alone."

"Ok, sleep well, I will be back in a couple of hours to check on you."

"Doug, what the fuck was that, oh my God, how is this woman a nurse? Am I overreacting?"

"I don't know babe, that was fucked up. I am going to stay tonight; you shouldn't be alone with her."

"No! You have to get back to Charlie, he isn't prepared for you to be gone all night."

"Ok, ok, you're right, but how about one more game?"

"Sure, if you don't mind losing." I said, slowly regaining my smile.

The next morning at shift change I told my new nurse of the experience from the night before and requested that the nurse I had last night never be put on my rotation again. She understood and mentioned they had a few complaints about her in the past.

That same morning, my doctor came in to check on me.

"Looks like that amoxicillin is working."

"Yep, I can feel it." I replied in a playful "told ya so" tone.

"You can feel it, hmm, well I am glad to see that you are getting better. We still have a long road; you were quite sick. Are you doing ok in here?"

"Not really, but I don't think I have much of a choice."

"Yeah, we are going to have to keep you a bit longer."

"How long, doc, I have already been here four days."

"I don't know, we have to pay attention to how your body is healing, but I would say another week or so."

"Really, another week, ugh!"

"Ok, I am going to check on some other patients. I will see you tomorrow. You tell your nurses if you notice anything or you start to feel worse instead of better, okay?"

"OK, thanks doc."

A few days before I went into the hospital, my mom was released from jail while she awaited trial. She made every effort to be with me when Doug couldn't. We didn't talk too much about what she was going through, it was more like for the first time, she really tried to take care of me. She brought me fresh juice every time she visited and helped me get some sunshine by dragging my IV outside with me. This, of course, was a bonus for her, too, because then she could smoke. She even ordered us take-out, so I didn't have to eat the hospital food...it was nice.

In a way, I thought it might actually be a fresh start. She had hit rock bottom, killing a man in her living room, and coming out of some of the hardest drugs she had ever used. I thought maybe she was ready for some true connection, but only time would tell.

After eleven days in the hospital, I had enough and begged the doctor to send me home. He was very reluctant, he wasn't seeing the progress and healing he wanted to release me. I reminded him that I was a healer, that I was sensitive to the stress of not trusting my caregivers (I continued to have a couple terrible nurses) and being in the hospital was preventing my full recovery.

For some reason he heard me, and he allowed me to go home, but I had to keep the central line in just in case I had to come back to the hospital. Later in my recovery he admitted that he did not expect me to recover at home and fully believed he would need that central line for emergency meds, which he didn't.

At home, surrounded by Charlie, my friends and nurtured with good food, I healed. My doc was happily surprised and other than a systemic yeast infection from all the antibiotics, I was ok.

A Fresh Start

Not long after our miscarriage, we found ourselves at the end of our lease in our current home. My mother very generously offered to put us up in her employee housing unit in downtown Aspen, we graciously accepted. Though the apartment was small, it had twelve-foot ceilings and floor-to-ceiling windows offering views of Aspen Mountain on one side and the backstage of The Wheeler Opera House through the other.

The only real drawback to the apartment was sleeping next to an alley with a large metal trash compactor for use by the entire block. At two every morning we would wake to the sound of bartenders from up and down the block dumping glass into the giant metal bin and then the bin crushing it. It was significantly disruptive.

We had a washing machine but no dryer, I hung our clothes up in the south-facing living room windows to dry. I found some sort of perverse satisfaction in hanging my undies in such prominent windows in downtown Aspen. It felt so very pedestrian in this egotistical town.

We were lucky to have this time in Aspen, it allowed us to save money and it allowed me to recover from all the medicine and hardship my body went through in the hospital. My mom was generous and didn't ask us to pay rent or utilities. She even chipped in some money to help update the apartment that was still sporting its original carpet and decor from the seventies. She was being incredibly kind, and we were immensely grateful, but our history meant that trust still did not come easily for me.

Chapter Seventeen

The Trial

It takes longer than I would expect to get a murder trial underway. Cody had been shot on June 27th, 2002, but the case didn't go to trial until August 2003. There was a good year where both the prosecution and the defense gathered evidence and worked out their cases. This meant that my mom had to relive the events that led to the shooting; the relationship, how it ended and the choices she made leading to that point. It couldn't have been easy, but my mom was holding it together pretty well, all things considered.

About a month after I got out of the hospital my mom and I met at a restaurant in Basalt where we could eat outside. We got a two top on the farthest corner of the deck, closest to the river and away from everyone else so we could talk freely.

Ironically, my healing office now sits above that same exact spot on the second floor of the same building. I think about this conversation often as I arrive to work.

"How are you holding up, mom?" I ask after the waitress takes our drink order.

"It's hard honey, it's so hard." She shook her head almost in disbelief.

"Do you miss him?" I ask in earnest.

"I do, but I am so glad he is gone." She replied through restrained tears. "I tried, ya' know, I tried to start over, to get him out of my life, but he just wouldn't leave me alone."

"When did you know he wasn't the big teddy bear anymore, when did he start to change?"

"I don't know Jessica, it's all kind of a blur. I have to remember so much for this trial, it's so hard."

"Did you love him?"

"Yes, you know I did..."

"Mom..." I am hesitant to ask the next question but my curiosity wins..." What does it feel like having killed a man?"

A tear escaped her eye as she whispered, "Impossible."

We pause our conversation as the waitress comes over to take our order. After she walks away my mom says, "He threatened to kill your brother Jessica." My mom had regained her composure.

"What...I mean how...I mean what?"

"Yes, he said he was going to kill me, then find Chad and beat him to within an inch of his life.

"Oh my God, I didn't know, I thought he came for money."

"Yeah, there is a lot you don't know, Jessica."

"Do you think he would have done that, like really kill you or Chad?"

"Of course, I do, that's why I shot him. I believed he was going to kill me right there in the living room. He wasn't ever going to go away, there was never going to be enough money, we were never going to be safe. He was going to kill me Jessica, he had gone crazy."

"Oh my God mom, of course, I am so sorry, it's just a lot, I can't imagine what you are feeling."

"He used to get angry when I wouldn't give him what he wanted and make me smoke meth or beat me senseless, sometimes both."

"Did Chad know?"

"He knew more than you, but not all of it, not how bad it got, he has his own stories with Cody."

Mom, why didn't you tell me?"

"I couldn't baby, I just couldn't. I finally got sick of it and asked him what it would take for him to go away and stay away."

"What did he tell you?"

"A hundred thousand dollars."

"Oh."

"I was so desperate to get him out of my life that I gave it to him."

"You gave him a hundred thousand dollars?!" I say this too loudly as I am in shock.

"Yes, all in cash... to leave us alone and let me start over. It only took him three months to come back for more...

three months! That's why he was there that morning, to demand more money...when I said I didn't have it, that's when he went nuts and started threatening me."

"Jesus mom, I had no idea, did he ever threaten to hurt me?"

"No, he always left you out of it, he used my relationship with Chad as a weakness."

"Do you think he ever loved you mom?"

"Yes."

"Me too. I am so sorry mom."

"At least he is gone now, I wish it hadn't happened this way, I wish he just would have left me alone. At least he can't hurt me anymore and your brother is safe."

Eventually, as the pressure from the impending trial started to unfold, so did my mom. She found her way back to drugs and drug dealers. She started making terrible decisions all over again and her addictions got the best of her. It was evident in her withdrawal, her weight loss and the light that was missing from her eyes.

We stopped meeting for lunch and the space between us grew once more.

Subtle Trauma

While standing in my neighbor Jessica's apartment one night I came across a deck of angel cards she had left out. I was visibly annoyed and moved them to the side.

"What's the problem there Jess?" Jessica asked in a teasing voice.

"Nothing, I just don't like cards."

"What do you mean you don't like cards?"

"I don't know, how can a deck of cards tell you anything, it's lame." I was short.

"Ok, ok, didn't know a deck of cards would set you off but whatever." Again, she was teasing me. Jessica was my saving grace in those first months in Aspen, I couldn't do much while my body was still healing. We enjoyed the same taste in music and generally had a similar life perspective, it was nice to have a friend just down the hall. "If cards can't tell you anything then just pull one for fun." It is clear she wasn't going to let up.

It had become a thing now, I had to pull one, so I did... the card was Child. "Huh? What does this even mean? I told you they don't work for me." It felt a little like adding insult to injury after just losing a child.

However, the cards did indeed work for me, just three days later, I found out I was pregnant again! The biggest surprise was that I was *able* to get pregnant. I was still healing from the antibiotics after the miscarriage and was blown away that my body wanted to hold and grow another child already; it had only been three months.

When I was pregnant with Bean, there were signs from the start that something was a little off. My urine tests never came back quite right, and I had developed a pencil eraser sized red spot just under my left eye. Though others may have overlooked something like that, after studying Chinese Medicine, I knew it was a sign of imbalance.

Although every test for this new pregnancy was coming

back perfect, the stress of what was going on in my family took its toll. It was enough that my mother was on trial for murder, but because she was a wealthy businesswoman in Aspen and Vail, the local newspapers covered her story regularly.

I walked Charlie every morning before grabbing a decaf and a paper from our local coffee shop. More times than I care to remember, there would be a front-page article about my mom titled things like; *"Local Furrier Kills Estranged Boyfriend"* or *"Sex Tape Leaked of Local Businesswoman with Man She Murdered"* or *"Airport Surveillance from Puerto Vallarta Shows Local Businesswoman Severely Beaten by Now Deceased Boyfriend"*.

This combined with knowing my mom was back down the rabbit hole of hard drugs made for a very stressful pregnancy.

Adding to the stress of the situation was my brother Chad's travels through Europe. He did his best to connect with us during daylight hours, but sometimes the phone would ring at odd times of night or very early in the morning. I was sure it was the police on the other end of the line telling me my mother had died of an overdose.

Perfect Union

Doug had asked me to marry him on a backpacking trip outside of Minturn just after we got pregnant with Bean. As we hiked, he walked behind me, picking long stalks of wild grasses that he eventually wove into an engagement ring.

We pitched our tent right next to Cross Creek about 50 yards from a waterfall so we could hear both the sound of the waterfall and the sound of the creek. The earth was soft there, cushioned with pine needles and the land was peaceful under the watch of two guardian Spruce Trees.

After a glorious night under the stars, Doug got up early, "Good morning sunshine, I am going to go on an early hike, you stay here and keep warm." he said giving me a quick kiss on the forehead before he left.

"No problem." I said sleepily, snuggling down into my bag.

After about an hour, Doug came back to the tent to get me. He had a sweet smile on his face, but it wasn't quite a smile, it was more of a light.

"Come with me." He said gently as he reached out his hand for mine.

"Where are we going?"

Doug did not reply, but instead led me to a large boulder sitting in the early morning sun. It was soft and worn from time with a bit of moss growing on its north side. The rock was large enough that I needed help to the top where Doug had laid out a flower crown for me in the first rays of sunlight that morning. I looked at it confused, but he just smiled as he took the crown and put it on top of my bald head (I had recently shaved off all my dreadlocks). He told me he had gotten up early to search for the most beautiful flowers in the forest to make me a flower crown, I was beside myself.

So there we sat, the sun pouring down warming our faces, me with a flower crown and him with a sweet smile, not a word spoken between us. He then turned to me and took my hand. Without hesitation, Doug presented me with the ring of wild grasses he had woven on the hike and asked me to spend the rest of my life with him...without hesitation, I accepted.

Doug and I have a creative synchronicity that plays well together, we tend to complement each other in most of our endeavors, naturally knowing our place, our strengths, and our practices. When our energy unfolds in creation, it is nothing short of magic, our wedding was no exception.

When it came time to plan our wedding, we agreed on just about everything; especially that it should be outside, we wanted to share this magical land with our family. We wanted to bring together all the uniqueness that was us. We designed and made our invitations and coordinated everything from the band to the food, together.

When we found out that I was pregnant again, we explored moving the wedding up to accommodate my growing belly. Ultimately though, we decided to keep it an autumn wedding; it was our favorite season, and we didn't want the stress of figuring everything out on a shortened schedule.

I was working at the Aspen Parks Department at the time and suggested we get married at John Denver Memorial Sanctuary. This was not some crazy obsession about John Denver, it's just this lovely outdoor area that lent itself perfectly to a wedding.

John Denver Memorial Sanctuary is a manmade outdoor amphitheater that appears as if it has always been there. It is nestled along a dirt path, footsteps from the headwaters of the Roaring Fork River, where the river still resembles a small creek.

There are two paths that climb from the river through a rock and flower garden to the site of the ceremony. Along the paths are eight-foot-tall rocks engraved with the lyrics of John Denver songs. The two paths meet on a sandstone platform at the bottom of a small hill with intentionally placed rocks, providing seating for the service.

As fate would have it, the woman in charge of renting the parks and all that goes along with it was named Karma (no joke). When I asked about park rentals, she handed me the standard pamphlet that let us know that renting John Denver Memorial Sanctuary would be several hundred dollars and renting a separate park where we would hold the reception would be another several hundred dollars. I sort of sighed as I was reading it, everything was starting to add up.

Hearing this, Karma looked up from her computer and said, "What are you looking to do?"

"I am getting married in September."

"Oh, how nice, what parks are you looking at?"

"John Denver for the ceremony and the one behind the Lenado for the reception, all our guests will be at the Lenado."

"That sounds lovely, how about $50 bucks each plus insurance?"

"What? That's not what it says here." I point to the pamphlet.

"That's ok, I got ya!"

"That is incredible, thank you so much, what do I need to fill out?"

"Just fill these things out, get me proof of insurance, and it's yours." She handed me the paperwork.

The wedding and reception came together beautifully. We had a husband and wife from Universal Unitarians perform the ceremony. He wore a purple velvet tux with tails and she, a beautiful purple dress, and a big floppy hat to shade her from the sun.

It was a perfect bluebird day, 76 degrees with a cool breeze that blew the aspen leaves around us like slow, floating confetti as if to celebrate our union.

Doug and I began barefoot in the headwaters of the Roaring Fork River, symbolizing purity and new beginnings. Then we made our way through the rock gardens, each taking our own path, before joining again in the sanctuary of the quaint sandstone platform surrounded by wildflowers, friends, and family.

Our groomsmen and bridesmaids proceeded us and Jake, Doug's nephew, led Charlie through the rock garden as our ring bearer.

Our pastors from Universal Unitarian greeted us and the guests before my maid of honor smudged Doug and me. The couple marrying us, and the entire space with white sage while I played the Native American flute. We incorporated a few more rituals before saying our vows, including Tibetan singing bowls and a Native American Prayer to the Four Directions.

Doug and I both wore white, I was in a flowery, white fairy gown that barely showed my six-month pregnant belly and Doug wore white hemp pants with a white Mexican wedding shirt. I had removed the white satin ribbon from the back of my dress and replaced it with blue, orange, and yellow ribbon, matching the flowers and ribbon in my flower crown. Doug wore a Hawaiian lei of white flowers around his neck while the groomsmen were in tan hemp pants with sage green Mexican wedding shirts with leis of orange and yellow. The ladies wore simple blue hemp dresses and held bouquets similar to mine. We were mirroring our natural world with green, blue, and orange which was surrounding us all on this incredible autumn day.

Our vows were full of gratitude and a commitment to lifting each other up. I never wrote anything down; I didn't need to; Doug was the first person to see and love all of me. There was so much light in how he saw me, I think I still looked at him in awe. It was hard to believe anyone could be that good.

The ceremony ended with Jeff Tweedy's *Mountain Bed*, played on a single violin, and sung by a friend of Doug's...it was perfect.

Once the ceremony was over, we all walked to the next park where the reception was being held on the back side of the boutique hotel where our guests were staying.

We hired a local Bluegrass band for the reception, and we danced our asses off amongst the falling leaves of autumn. There was an ease in the whole experience.

Our dear friend ordered us a whole fresh Salmon through his restaurant, and we hired a local chef to grill it along with some veggies, rice, and salad, right there in the park, it was a simple but perfect meal.

The cake was three layers, vanilla cake with custard and raspberry. The woman who made it was in complete alignment with the whole celebration and even dried colorful aspen leaves to lay over the top for decoration.

The sun had not yet set when we called it a day, but the day had been long and full. We retired in our room with its own mountain bed made of twigs and branches bent into swirls to make a canopy above us. Our friends had spelled "make beautiful love" on the bed with autumn leaves. We laid there together in perfection, feeling the vibration of so much joy shared on our behalf and felt complete.

There were, of course, concerns along the way, mainly that my mom wouldn't make it and if she made it, would she be sober, or was she going to cause a scene? Gratefully, she held it together enough to make it to our wedding, seemingly sober and celebratory. This was great to see but I can tell you that there were many days when that didn't seem possible.

The Homebirth That Wasn't

When I went into labor, I called my midwife, Jules. She assured me that the contractions were far enough apart that I had some time and to call her when they got closer.

Jules had become a close friend after we shared our first office space in Carbondale, both of us just starting our practices and only needing a few days a week at the time. I would have had no idea that homebirth was an option had she not been my officemate, but after meeting her and getting some basic education, I knew it was the right choice for me.

Jules and I were pregnant together and she had given

birth a month earlier to a beautiful baby girl named Stella. She had set up a good support team for her and Stella while she attended my labor; her mother and husband taking turns bringing Stella to us to nurse every 2 to 4 hours for the entirety of my twenty-four-hour labor.

It was incredibly beautiful and inspiring to be so near to what I was trying to bring into the world.

We were set up for success at home with a huge birthing tub that practically took up our whole living room and several George Winston CDs to set the mood. I had good snacks around in case the labor ran long, and I had all the baby's stuff put away, ready to go. Standing in my living room, looking around at the scene to come, I remember thinking, "I've got this...I think we're ready."

The lack of understanding I had about labor was laughable. I couldn't fucking eat in the middle of it, and I didn't even hear the music. The birthing tub, however, was a life saver, it took just enough pressure off to allow me to move through the contractions, unfortunately it relaxed me a bit too much. Jules said in order to make progress I was going to have to get out and move around. Six hours went by and although my contractions were hard and close, I wouldn't open, and baby wouldn't budge.

Twelve hours go by; and aside from listening to a shit ton of George Winston, we are in the same place. After eighteen hours, still not much has changed, my cervix hadn't opened, and my water still hadn't broke.

"Honey," Jules says as she gently moves my hair out of my face, "I know you don't want to hear this, but we need to go to the hospital."

"No way, I am not going, they are fucking idiots!" I am clear about this after my previous miscarriage experience.

"My love, this is a different situation, a different hospital, we need to go, your baby isn't coming, we need some assistance."

"Please don't make me go, Jules please… Doug, tell her, I won't go!"

"Jess, if Jules says it's time, then it's time, she is trying to help us." Doug is kind, he is sensitive to the fact I didn't want to go to the hospital, but he knows Jules is right.

"Honey my job is to make sure you and your baby are healthy; I can't do anything else to help you and your baby isn't coming. For the safety and health of both of you, we need to transfer. Doug, why don't you walk Charlie, I will get some things together and we will go when you get back." Jules is serious now and taking charge.

"Jules please, isn't there anything else, can't we wait longer?" I beg.

"No Jess, it's time, I am sorry, I know this isn't what you wanted."

To our surprise, Aspen Valley Hospital was both respectful and kind. We had interrupted their Christmas party, the doctor on call was wearing a festive red and white sweater with Santa's sleigh and reindeer embroidered on it. She was in a cheery mood, not showing she was put out at all by us crashing their party. She even demonstrated great respect for Jules and invited her to catch the baby when the time came.

But the time was not coming, I continued not to make progress and it was determined that I would be given pitocin. Pitocin was a terrible experience for me, sure it helped move along the labor, but the contractions became hard, edgy, and much more difficult to move through. It was an appropriate intervention in appropriate timing, but it still sucked.

I went from laboring in the privacy of my home with my own music and ability to move around to laboring in the hospital under fluorescent lights with several people I didn't know standing around watching me. There was a monitor hooked to my belly and an IV in my arm, I was tethered, and I hated it.

Even with pitocin, I made little progress, our baby just wouldn't come down.

Finally, after two more hours had passed in hard labor with little progress, they took me into surgery and prepped for a C section. But the doctor paused, knowing our wishes, and opted to try suction and forceps first. After three tries with the suction the doctor switched to forceps, with one firm grab and pull, out came our beautiful baby girl.

Unlike today's gender reveal enthusiasts, we didn't know what we were going to have and were excited for the surprise.

Emma Nepal Jacobson didn't cry when she was born; her eyes were wide open, looking around, but she didn't cry. Even as they suctioned her nose and cleaned her off, she stayed relatively calm. They gave her to me for just a moment before they took her to clean her up. She was small, 5lbs 9oz, but long at 22 inches.

As I write this, I can reflect on what I saw when she was born and perhaps give an explanation as to why she didn't cry. Her spirit was not fully in her body yet, I see now that she was unsure about coming in, like she second guessed her choice to incarnate. There has been much in her now seventeen-year-old life that has demonstrated this, and we have often noted the parallel of her unwillingness to be born to her unwillingness to live. In fact, I find my children's birth stories are a good representation of who they are in life or their personalities if you will.

Doug held her in his arms just after she got cleaned up when the doctor wanted to move her to lay under a special light.

"Let us have the baby Mr. Jacobson."

"No, I've got her, I can follow you."

"I am sorry Mr. Jacobson; we need to transport her in this." Pointing to an infant bed on wheels. "It's for liability sir, you can't carry her."

"Well then I guess she is staying right here, because I am not letting her go."

The doctor realized Doug wasn't going to budge, it wasn't that Doug was being difficult, it's that he was in love with this little girl, it was his job to keep her safe and he just wasn't going to let her go.

"Ok sir, follow me."

Doug disappeared with our daughter in his arms, and I was left with Jules as they sewed me up. Once they wheeled me into recovery, Jules too had to go home to her own baby, Stella. She must have been exhausted, being a new mom and holding space for a twenty-four-hour labor. Jules had kept me safe through the worst of times; first when I miscarried Bean and now by keeping our baby and I safe throughout this entire labor, even when I didn't want to cooperate. She will forever be my hero.

So there I lay, in a very small, sterile room by myself, watching the clock. I still couldn't feel my legs, the nurse had said it might take an hour or so for them to wake up and not to worry, then she closed the door on her way out. Ten minutes went by, no one came to check on me or tell me where or how my family was. Then thirty minutes...I still couldn't feel my legs...*was anyone going to check on me? Had I been forgotten?* Never in my life have I felt as alone as I did laying in that hospital bed after giving birth. The separation felt counterintuitive breaking an understood sacred bond between mother and child.

After an hour, a nurse came to wheel me into a hospital room where my family was waiting. It was already one in the morning, and I still couldn't feel my legs, we had been up almost thirty-two hours straight. After only a hug, Doug passed out on the bed next to mine while Emma Nepal nursed before falling asleep in my arms. I wasn't willing to wake her up or risk moving, so I held her there, contently watching her sleep for nearly four hours before a nurse came to check on us. She was able to take our baby and put her gently in her infant bed next to mine without waking her. I got only three hours of sleep before the next round of nurses came in around seven.

"Good morning, Jessica, how are you feeling today?" asked a chipper nurse.

"I feel pretty good, I am tired though."

"I bet, sounds like it was quite an adventure! Did you get any sleep?"

"No."

"Are you in any pain?"

241

"I don't think so, I haven't really moved from this bed since the birth."

"Ok, love, well it's time to try, you have had quite a lot of trauma downstairs and we need to see if you can go to the bathroom."

"What do you mean, I might not be able to go to the bathroom?!"

"Come on honey, let's get you standing up."

At this point Doug startles awake and can't quite remember where he is. "What, what's going on?"

"Good morning my love, they are asking me to try to move around a bit to see if there is any pain."

"Oh my God babe, that was crazy what happened to you last night, how can I help?"

"Will you just help me up?" Just shifting positions on the bed to a more upright seated position told me I was going to have pain.

They had kept me on pain medicine all through the night and I didn't understand what had really happened to my body, but Doug had seen the whole thing and he seemed to think it was a miracle I was moving at all.

"Ok, babe, hold my hands and I will help you up." Doug planted himself in front of me with a wide legged stance for stability. I began to bear weight, and so far, it felt ok. My yoni (yoni is Sanskrit for opening, it's what we call our female genitalia, it's just a prettier word than vagina) felt like it was three sizes too big and hard as a rock, but my pain was manageable.

"I got it; I think I can move around on my own." I started to walk around the small hospital room, I was careful, a little hunched over, but I was ok.

"Ok Jessica, it's time to go to the bathroom." The nurse chirped as though I was a dog, or I could go on command.

"Um, ok."

"I am going to come in here with you and watch, you have a lot of stitches, and we need to make sure everything is working properly."

"What? How might everything not work properly?" I ask, terrified of the answer.

"Let's just try to go to the bathroom shall we and then we can cross the next bridge if we need to."

Sitting down on the toilet was no easy task, it was lower than the bed, so naturally, I engaged my pelvic muscles, but they wouldn't engage, and I just about fell down.

"Oh my God, what is going on?"

"Calm down, does it feel ok to sit down?" asked the nurse.

"NO!" "What happened to me? What's going on?"

"Do you want to touch it? That might help you understand, I could get you a mirror so you can see what it looks like down there."

"Yeah ok, get me a mirror, I can't pee right now, this is insane!"

"No, no don't pee yet, we need to flush your area with this alkaline water while you are going to the bathroom, so it doesn't hurt as much."

"What? Please, just get me the mirror."

"Here you go, nice and easy ok, it's ok." the nurse says as she passes me the hand mirror.

"Oh my God, what happened, oh my God." I broke into tears.

What I see in the mirror doesn't resemble any kind of human anatomy. I look more like a Ken doll of swollen scar tissue with huge green zigzagged stitches running from my ass to my clitoris. This was not me; how would this heal?

"Jess, honey, are you ok in there? Do you want me to help?" Doug calls from the other room.

"No, no…. no…no, I don't understand."

In order to make room for forceps, the doctor cut my perineum, but because of the forceps, I tore a rectal muscle as well as split my skin all the way up to my clitoris.

"Ok, ok, ok, can I touch it?"

"You should probably wash your hands first."

"No way am I getting off this toilet just to sit back down, ok I have to pee, should I try?"

"We need to make sure you spray this bottle of water the whole time you are urinating ok, can you do that?"

"I need to hold and squeeze a bottle of water on myself while I pee?"

"Yes, do you want me to do it for you this first time?"

"Yes please, it's all just too much."

"Ok, tell me when."

"Now I think."

"OH MY GOD, AHHH…FUCK!"

"It's ok honey, you got it."

"That hurts so bad, why does it hurt like that?"

"You have fresh stitches and urine is acidic. It's going to hurt like that for about a week. The water that we spray while you are urinating cuts the acidity, can you imagine if you didn't do that?"

"Oh my God, a week?! Oh my God, what am I going to do?

"It will get better every day, honey, you are going to be alright, you will need to pay attention to going number two though, you tore right through a rectal muscle, it might be a little dicey for a while until you regain control."

"What do you mean, until I regain control? Are you saying I might shit myself?"

"Let's not worry about that now, it will be a few days before your body is even ready to poop. Take it one day at a time."

After some help up off the toilet, it was time to nurse. Emma Nepal had been starting to fuss in the other room. I shuffled over to her, still reeling from the experience of going to the bathroom and seeing what had happened to my yoni, but my child was calling.

Doug was holding Emma Nepal, moving her back and forth while gazing lovingly at her when I came up next to him. He turned and looked at me with pain and concern in his eyes for what I was going through. He was present for me, but he also felt helpless, so much of right now was on me, but just knowing that he would have done it all for me if he could, was everything.

"Jessica, why don't you get back in the bed then we can hand you your daughter and you can try to nurse."

"No way am I sitting back down, I've got her." Doug handed me our daughter and the next part felt natural. Emma Nepal latched right away, just as she had last night. The lactation consultant kept trying to help by moving my breast upwards, but I just found her to be in the way. I could feel there was colostrum coming out, and she was clearly swallowing it.

Jules arrived back at the hospital just as we started nursing and the other two nurses left out of respect giving us privacy. "Oh my gosh honey, look at her, how are you feeling, Doug, did you get any sleep?" Jules said, shoving three sentences into one.

"We are ok, um, did you see what they did to me?"

"Yeah honey, I know it's so hard, how are you feeling today?"

"Um, not great!"

"Still, I think it's better that you had a vaginal birth, it means if you have another baby, you can try for another homebirth and aren't forced to do a C-section. Your doctor was very respectful of us, I don't see that a lot."

"That's great I guess, but fuck, I am really torn up down there, it's not ok."

The hospital let us go by ten o'clock that morning. In the end, I wasn't even there for twelve hours.

It was wonderful to be home; though getting up the stairs was hard; I knew my Charlie would be waiting for me. He was so happy to see us and meet our new baby. He was looking at her, then looking at me while his butt wiggled back and forth constantly threatening to knock something over. He was naturally sweet and gentle with her but stayed right with me all the time, making sure I was ok just as he had done while I labored at home. Even when Doug went to take him out, he looked back at me to make sure it was ok that he left, he was such a good dog.

We could see out our kitchen window a big sign that read **Welcome to The World Emma Nepal!** It was made by my mother and put in the back window of her fur store that faced our apartment. She had apparently spent the night there, waiting for us to get home.

I wasn't quite ready to see her, we knew she had been using profusely the last few months, our wedding was the last time she was seen clean and sober. But whether I liked it or not, she was there, excited to greet us and meet her new granddaughter. She could see us through the window, and we could see her, I couldn't tell her to go away so Doug gave her a call to invite her over.

"Do you guys need anything? I could go to the grocery store." Mom said excitedly over the phone.

"No Kathy, we are good, come on up and meet the baby." Doug encouraged.

When my mom arrived, two minutes later, she looked homeless. She was scrawny and pale with sores on her face, but there was light in her eyes, light because she was so excited to meet this little girl.

We couldn't quite tell if she was sober, but she was being

really kind, talking at a regular pace and showing incredible respect toward us. We sat her in a big blue chair with tall, cushioned arms before we handed her the baby. She beamed with joy, like Doug, my mom was truly in awe of this sweet little girl.

After about an hour, my mom decided to make a grocery run for us. We didn't ask her to, but it was clear she couldn't sit still, she was probably high, yet still well meaning. This break gave us time to settle in and really look at our baby for the first time in privacy.

She was perfect, but the whole ordeal was traumatic for us all, probably most for Emma Nepal, though we didn't understand that at the time. I can't imagine being brought into the world with my first experience of matter being metal spoons tugging at my head.

Those metal spoons were no friend of mine either and the first week home was brutal. I took my first shower a day after we got home. It had been difficult at best just to pee, and I was nervous about taking a shower and getting more familiar with my yoni. I went through the motions in the shower, washing my hair, under my armpits and such before I cautiously touched myself where I had given birth. It was a hard mound of torn up tissue, my yoni did not feel part of me, but instead like a foreign entity that had taken over my body. I sobbed and sobbed; I couldn't imagine how this would heal.

Doug had only three days off work to spend with us before he had to go back. We spent those days staring at our baby and sleeping. He did everything possible to make sure I was well taken care of including getting up in the middle of the night when Emma Nepal needed to nurse. There wasn't much he could do to support me in those first few days, but he wanted to.

"Go back to bed my love, you can't help me here." I whispered in his ear as he bent over me to catch a glimpse of our daughter.

"I don't want you to have to do it alone, if you're up, I am up!"

"I love you so much for this Doug, but really, I will do these early years and when she is a teenager and she hates me I will send her off into the woods with you, deal?"

"Deal." So off to bed he went, little did we know at the time how true this statement would become.

Cliff Jumping

Not long after our daughter's birth and still in the middle of the murder trial, my mom got a DUI, was put on house arrest and forced to wear an ankle monitor. My brother was back from Europe and took on the duty of babysitting her as it was clear that left to her own devices she was going to overdose and not even make it to the trial. I was hopeful that Chad being home might help bring her back to family and possibly sobriety but one day, when Emma Nepal was about two months old, my brother called.

"Jess, I am driving around looking for mom, she took off with Geno."

"Isn't she on house arrest? What is going to happen if she breaks house arrest? Wait, why did she take off?" I was confused and trying to get orientated with the information.

"Look Jess, I don't know about any of that, but I just saw Geno running down the road half naked, he told me I should probably go look for her."

"Wait, what?"

"House arrest isn't going to matter much if she is dead in a ditch Jess. Geno said she might be at the bottom of some cliffs that are out on the old road heading toward the rodeo grounds."

"Oh my God, what is going on, ok, do you need any help, I mean...I guess I can drive up there, but I have Emma Nepal."

"No Jess, this is rough, you shouldn't have your baby here. But look, from what I heard from Geno, you should be prepared, this is probably going to be ugly, sounds like they jumped off those cliffs just below I-70 for some reason, I am going to see if I can find her or her car."

"Ok brother, I am so sorry you have to do this. I don't know what to say...what does Geno have to do with any of this?"

"Geno has been getting her drugs since Cody left, remember that fucked up Christmas? That was all Geno. Honestly this is just par for the course. I'm just not sure she is going to come out of this one alive.... I will call you later after I find her, bye."

"Bye." I hung up the phone dumbfounded, what did Chad even say, my mom jumped off a cliff with Geno naked.... that can't be right.

Unfortunately, that's exactly what happened, Chad found my mom at the base of a cliff, naked, right where Geno had said she would be. She was passed out when he found her but other than a few bumps, scrapes and bruises, she was fine.

Chad brought her back to the house and tried to clean her up before having to go out to find her car, which was sitting on the side of I-70 with the passenger door still wide open. He needed a break; this was too much for him day in and day out, so he asked me to come for a day to take care of her. I understood and felt compassion, I told him I would come the next day.

Aspen is about an hour and a half away from Eagle, so it wasn't a big deal, except I had a brand-new baby that I was reluctant to expose to this very unstable situation.

Chad was anxious when I arrived, waiting at the door for me like a caged animal about to be freed. "Don't let her leave the house, she is high as fuck, people are bringing her drugs, don't let anyone in." He was stern.

"What? Ok, can't we just call the police or something?"

"Then she will get more jail time, this doesn't help her case Jess, you know it was self-defense but if she is seen as an out-of-control addict, she will lose the case." Chad was right, I hadn't thought it all the way through. "Have Fun, she's not dangerous, she is just kind of like a drunk teenage girl...it gets tiring." Then he left.

Upon entering the house, I found my mother high as a fucking kite, wearing a black lace teddy laying in front of the fire.

Seeing my mom like this was heartbreaking, I experienced emotions of disgust, pity, outrage, and sadness all in a single breath.

When my mom saw me come in, she was ecstatic! "Jessica, oh this is such a nice surprise! Did you bring my granddaughter to see me?" She got off the floor and came towards me.

I took a step back, "Mom, why are you wearing that? Come on, put some clothes on!"

"Oh, who cares honey, sometimes a girl wants to feel pretty."

"I care, it's weird to see your mom in a teddy, please go put some clothes on."

"Ok, Ok, but first, let me hold my granddaughter."

"Mom, you are high as fuck on I don't even know what, you know I can't let you hold her."

"You know Jessica, that is probably best, I understand. If the situation were reversed, I wouldn't let you hold my baby either. Ok, I will put on some clothes."

My entire day was spent playing defense. She was very much like a drunk girl, talking in circles, wanting to dance, or run across the yard naked, it was fucking awful.

When my brother got back at four o'clock, I too was ready to get out of there. "Dude, what the fuck is going on with her, do you know what kind of drugs she is taking?"

"I don't know Jess, it's rough, I think people are like leaving shit in flowerpots when I take a shower. She has her phone, so she signals them or something, I don't know what the fuck she is on, I don't see her smoking anything so maybe pills, I don't know."

"No shit it's rough, how are you doing this Chad?"

"I gotta, who else is going to do it?"

"Maybe no one, I mean she has made a pretty shitty bed for herself, perhaps she should lie in it."

"I can't Jess, I just can't." Chad was committed, he loved her so much...but to be there day in and day out...I couldn't have done it.

Chapter Eighteen

Letting Go

Eventually, as the date for the trial drew closer, my mom started to pull her shit together. I imagine she was still doing drugs, but she was managing her addiction. We weren't talking a lot; I just couldn't bear to hear her broken and hollow voice on the other end of the line pretending she was fine. I did my best to support her, but I had a new baby to focus on and that was holding my attention beautifully.

It is around this time that Charlie stopped acting like himself; he had started scavenging around looking for food every time we went out. He was obsessive about it, his attention was more on scrounging for food than walking with me or playing with other dogs, it was very unlike him. Not long after his behavior change, he began throwing up several times a day. At first, I thought it was due to all the junk he was eating off the ground, but after three days, we took him to the vet where it was determined that Charlie had cancer of the spleen, common for Golden Retrievers. There wasn't much to be done, he was going to die in the next month or two. We got him some medicine to help with the vomiting and make him more comfortable, but the love of my life was dying, and nothing was going to change that.

The first morning waking up to our new reality I sat on the edge of the bed and cried. Doug held my hand, but there was nothing that was going to make the hurt go away. Charlie saved my life, I really believe that I was heading down the wrong path when he showed up and shined his light on me. We saved each other and now...there was nothing I could do but let him go. I wasn't ready, what about Emma Nepal, she wasn't even going to get to know him!

My mother's trial began in the midst of Charlie's declining health. She was doing a decent job presenting herself as a successful businesswoman that acted in self-defense, but it was hard on her. After a brutal ten days of testimony, where the prosecution did their best to smear her character (which wasn't terribly difficult), she was acquitted of manslaughter, the jury ruling she shot Cody in self-defense.

Finally, after more than a year, it was over. Local papers from Vail to Aspen again covered the story in greater detail than I would have liked, but at least it gave me an objective glimpse into what had happened. There was more to the story than my mom had told me, mostly gruesome details of his regular assaults on her and the premeditative rage he was in when he reached the ranch. Cody had been bragging to people around town about how he was going to kill her...even telling people that were close to her, like her dentist where he had been the morning of the shooting. It was almost like he wanted someone to stop him, because he knew he couldn't stop himself...

The Last Light

I knew I wanted to soak up every last moment with Charlie, so I bundled Emma Nepal up in a sling and zipped an oversized down jacket around us so we could walk as long as Charlie wanted on any given day.

I had been in touch with my mother after the trial, she had been sober since it began, maybe thirty days at this point and I told her what was happening with Charlie, she understood. She said she would take care of everything when the time was right.

Within a few weeks Charlie grew tired, he no longer wanted to take long walks, then he didn't want to take any walks at all, it eventually became difficult to get him outside just to go to the bathroom. The writing was on the wall; he wagged his tail when we came home but when he stopped getting up to greet us, we knew it was time. His food had started to go unwanted and even his water sat stagnant in his bowl, he was showing us he was ready.

I made the call to my mom, three days later we loaded Charlie up in the truck and drove to the ranch. She had prepared a grave and had her veterinarian waiting for us. When we took Charlie out of the truck, we noticed his energy was quite good and he seemed to be acting like his old self. The Chinese call this the last light; it's an opportunity to say goodbye to our loved ones and experience the glory of life one last time, we knew this meant he was close to letting go.

We watched with joy as Charlie ran around the yard like a puppy, but then as if there was a flick of a switch, he was done and came over to sit next to us, revealing the tired old dog he truly was. After Doug and I gave Charlie a full body rub, we walked nearer to his grave and he followed, he knew what was to come. I got down on the ground with him, he laid his head on my lap. My mom held Emma Nepal while Doug and I said our goodbyes and as the injection went in, we felt his spirit leave and his body was left empty.

Charlie went easily, he was ready, and he knew I was in good hands with Doug. Charlie was my best friend, my most loyal companion and my angel of light. Charlie went by many names; Charlie Tuna, Charlie Bucket, Charlie Dog but most commonly, Charlie Pants. He brought joy to all who knew him and peace to my heart, I couldn't believe he was gone.

Doug and I lowered him into the grave and covered him with dirt. It was a good ending, as good as one could get under the circumstances but an ending just the same.

"Thank you, mom, you have made a very difficult thing a little easier."

"I know baby, I am so sorry."

"Kathy, thank you so much, this means the world to us." Doug still had tears in his eyes and his voice was shaky. He leaned in and gave her a gentle hug, wrapping one arm around Emma Nepal as he held them both.

It was time to leave, after one last look at Charlie's grave, I turned to my mother and took back my child, she would now be my *soul's* focus.

About Jess Jacobson

Jess Jacobson is a Healer, Psychic Medium and Spiritual Teacher that lives with her above average husband, three eccentric kids and two dogs in the mountains of Colorado. Her life's service has been helping others remember self-love, spiritual purpose and connection.

Jess's Divine message of love and connection breaks through all barriers, allowing the truth of each person to unfold. As we open to self-love, we allow for greater personal responsibility in creating the life we are meant to live.

Jess's specialty is working with Intergenerational Trauma through multiple generations. Honoring that even those who have passed can participate in this process, clearing the way for those still with us today and generations to come.

Please keep your eyes peeled for, ***To Love Like a River, A mother's resistance to deep pain and even deeper love.*** The second book in this series...*and thank you for your support!*

May you find perseverance in self-love, personal

responsibility, and spiritual purpose, remember, Life's the School, Love's the Lesson!

About The Cover Designer

Faren Wilbur is a creative born and raised on the Western Slope of Colorado. Faren attended Colorado Mesa University where she received a BFA in Animation, Film, Photography and Motion Design and a minor in Art. Her Grandmother introduced her to drawing and gave Faren her first tin of crayons. Her mother supported all her creative endeavors and was a huge inspiration. A majority of Faren's compositions are influenced by the natural beauty that is found on the Western Slope and nature in general. Faren wants to convey how she sees the world through her work and share her knowledge of creating with others. When Faren isn't creating, she loves hiking, exploring ghost towns, traveling, and spending time with her family.

Made in the USA
Las Vegas, NV
02 October 2021

31465478R00144